A Handbook for Teaching Assistants

This revised new edition provides essential guidance for all teaching assistants, especially those who are new to the job, and to the teachers working with them. Glenys Fox details the roles and responsibilities of the TA, as well as providing helpful advice on how to best support the teacher, the pupil, the curriculum and the school. This practical handbook will bring experienced TAs up to date on changes to national educational guidance, including changes in the national curriculum, assessment and the special educational needs framework.

This text enables the assistant and the teacher to work together more effectively in supporting and promoting the progress of children and young people. Written in light of recent research and updates in legislation, this guide will ensure that:

- teaching assistants know what to expect of colleagues, and vice versa
- pupils are given the best possible support by teaching assistants who understand their needs
- teaching assistants and teachers are able to work together effectively to support the learning of all children, especially children who have special educational needs and disabilities
- any training received is relevant and helpful.

A Handbook for Teaching Assistants is an ideal textbook for training, as well as a useful classroom handbook for teaching assistants working in early years, primary and secondary settings.

Glenys Fox is an education consultant. She has taught in mainstream and special settings and was a Principal Educational Psychologist before joining Ofsted as an HMI (Her Majesty's Inspector of Schools).

A Handbook for Teaching Assistants

Teachers and assistants working together

Third edition

Glenys Fox

Routledge
Taylor & Francis Group

LONDON AND NEW YORK

This edition published 2017
by Routledge
2 Park Square, Milton Park, Abingdon, Oxon OX14 4RN

and by Routledge
711 Third Avenue, New York, NY 10017

Routledge is an imprint of the Taylor & Francis Group, an informa business

First edition published in 1998 by David Fulton Publishers

British Library Cataloguing in Publication Data
A catalogue record for this book is available from the British Library

Library of Congress Cataloging in Publication Data
Names: Fox, Glenys.
Title: A handbook for teaching assistants: teachers and assistants working together/ Glenys Fox.
Description: 3rd edition. | New York: Routledge, 2017. | Includes bibliographical references.
Identifiers: LCCN 2016004566 | ISBN 9781138126190 (handbook: alk. paper) | ISBN 9781138126206 (pbk.) | ISBN 9781315647029 (ebook)
Subjects: LCSH: Teachers' assistants—Great Britain—Handbooks, manuals, etc. | Special education—Great Britain—Handbooks, manuals, etc.
Classification: LCC LB2844.1.A8 F68 2017 | DDC 371.14/1240941—dc23
LC record available at http://lccn.loc.gov/2016004566

ISBN: 978-1-138-12619-0 (hbk)
ISBN: 978-1-138-12620-6 (pbk)
ISBN: 978-1-315-64702-9 (ebk)

Typeset in Bembo
by Deanta Global Publishing Services, Chennai, India

I dedicate this new edition to David Fulton, an inspirational publisher who championed the first published books for teaching assistants.

Contents

Acknowledgements

I am indebted to all those assistants who have contributed to my research into their role and training needs. Much inspiration has come from their dedication to and care of some of our most needy children and young people. Thanks to the teachers and assistants at The Mountbatten School Romsey, Lymington C.E. Infant School and Lymington Junior School for their observations.

Glenys Fox

January 2016

Purpose

The purpose of this handbook is to enable teaching assistants to work more effectively in supporting:

- the learning and development of children and young people;
- the class teacher;
- the curriculum;
- the school.

Audience

This handbook is intended as a resource for:

- all teaching assistants (learning support assistants, special needs assistants, early years assistants, bilingual assistants);
- teachers, senior managers, inclusion managers and special needs coordinators who manage assistants;
- those who run training courses for assistants (college lecturers, SENCOs).

Overview

There are sections on:

- the current context and statutory frameworks;
- roles and responsibilities;
- promoting effective learning;
- giving support;
- the range of additional and special needs;
- working with colleagues to support learning.

Introduction

It is 23 years since the publication of my first book for teaching assistants, written because there were few sources of information available for assistants. At that time most assistants were known as Special Needs Assistants or Learning Support Assistants.

The book was received enthusiastically by assistants and schools. I have been really encouraged by the response to that original book and to my subsequent books. Although the nature of children and young people has not changed since then, the cultural and political world around them *has* moved on, and the influences on their lives and on schools *have* changed. The job of the teaching assistant has broadened and diversified so that they are now employed in a wider range of roles in many different educational settings.

Now is a good time to revisit the handbook and update the contents to reflect the changes in legislation and technology which are currently influencing the roles of assistants in our schools. Of course there are some things that don't change, such as the importance of developing confidence in children and young people as learners, and the nature of some special educational needs, which require the sensitive support of assistants.

However, there have been significant changes for teaching assistants (TAs), who are now recognised as an important and indispensable resource in our schools. Many teachers say that they cannot work without them. Many children and young people gain much from their support. There is recognition from the government that the current school landscape is now very different. There has been an increasing focus on raising standards in schools and, as a result, assistants need to be more aware of and informed about their role in promoting effective learning.

There are now more TAs in our schools, and the numbers continue to grow, indicating the value of assistants in supporting schools. In the year 2000, there were 79,000 TAs, and by 2014 this number had more than tripled to 255,100. A quarter of the workforce in mainstream schools in England is comprised of TAs; 34 per cent of nursery and primary school staff; and 15 per cent of secondary school staff. In addition, there are over 30,000 assistants working in special schools (*Department for Education School Workforce Data 2014*).

There are many different types of teaching assistants, working at all levels and across all phases of education: preschool, infant, junior, secondary, special and further education. Some give general classroom support, some work in curriculum areas, some support groups of children who need extra help to make progress and some work with individual pupils who have significant learning needs or medical conditions.

The importance of giving support and guidance to assistants is clear. They are frequently working closely with some very needy children and young people whose quality of school experience can depend quite significantly on the teaching assistant's knowledge and skills. In addition, a good deal of skilled expertise goes into assessment and describing the needs and type of provision for pupils who need learning support. It follows that the delivery of any learning described in individual learning programmes should be carried out by teachers working in partnership with assistants who have had appropriate and relevant training. A publication by the Education Endowment Foundation concerning the best use of teaching assistants (2015) indicates that, where training and guidance is clear, TAs can support pupils with learning difficulties very effectively. However, too often TAs are expected to take on more responsibility for the work with pupils with learning difficulties than the teacher, who in fact retains the main responsibility for their learning. This is an issue which some schools have not yet addressed.

There are now more opportunities for training – a positive change. In fact it has become, quite rightly, more professional. Teaching assistants need good quality training and support to do their jobs well. However, there is still a need to provide equal nationwide access to, and funding for, professional development. The responsibility for supporting assistants on a day-to-day basis lies primarily with class teachers and often with special needs coordinators (SENCOs). Head teachers have a key role to play by managing school staffing arrangements to free up time and funding for both planning and training.

This handbook is intended as a practical guide containing useful information which TAs and their teacher colleagues need to know. It can also be used to complement training courses. It includes information about the latest research into how teachers and assistants can work together effectively, the new national curriculum and the SEN Code of Practice published by the Department for Education in 2015, which provides guidance for schools to use in making arrangements for meeting children's special educational needs.

Since the first edition of this book, which was published in 1993, much has changed in the way assistants are seen in terms of the education workforce. The Special Educational Needs and Disability Act (SENDA 2001) and the revised Code of Practice (2001) promoted a greater degree of inclusion for children with a wide range of additional needs and disabilities, leading to many children who had been previously educated in special schools being included in mainstream schools. This has meant that teachers and assistants need to have a greater level of knowledge and skills with regard to the range of learning needs that they may encounter.

Although there have been changes in frameworks, legislation and processes over the last 20 years, and technology has improved, the minds of children and young people have not changed! Although we may be better now at understanding how children learn, and there are improved resources to support learning, the essential elements of good support remain unchanged. This book sets out the key ways in which assistants can promote the best learning. It highlights the valuable role that assistants play in the 'front line' of meeting children's day-to-day learning needs. It describes how the resource of an assistant can be managed well at school level and used to best effect when working in partnership with teachers to promote academic, social and emotional progress.

So, if you are a teaching assistant or intend to become one, or if you are a teacher working with an assistant, a SENCO or a school manager, then this handbook will help you in fulfilling your particular learning support role.

CHAPTER 1

The role of the teaching assistant

Chapter summary

- Possible roles
- What are my responsibilities?
- Which pupils might I be asked to support?
- What if something goes wrong?
- What support can I expect?
- What might I be asked to do?
- Specific tasks
- What are the ground rules?
- What do TAs enjoy about the role?
- What do TAs find difficult about the role?
  - Working with pupils
  - Working with teachers
  - Pay and conditions
- How has the role changed over recent years?
- Activity

'It's a fantastic job! Always different every day.'

(infant school TA)

'It is a very rewarding and worthwhile role. I enjoy working with the teachers and the children.'

(junior school TA)

'I love every second of my job.'

(secondary school TA)

Teaching assistants (TAs) have many different roles and the range of responsibilities has widened in recent times. If you work as a TA, you will know that it can be rewarding and worthwhile. It can also be frustrating at times! Most TAs enjoy their work and feel that they are making a positive difference to the lives of children and young people. Here are some more examples of what they say:

> 'Being a TA is a fantastic job. You get to meet all different kinds of children and to use your imagination on a daily basis. It's great fun and hard work, but very rewarding.'
>
> *(junior school TA)*

> 'The greatest reward is when a 'stroppy' Year 11 student comes and finds you when they leave and thanks you for all your help and support. That is what makes it all worthwhile.'
>
> *(secondary school TA)*

Starting out as an assistant can be daunting at first, but you will find that most teachers and assistants in your school will be very happy to help you learn about your role and, in most schools, there are good and supportive relationships in TA teams.

> 'I am very lucky to work with a great team who are always happy to help you with anything.'
>
> *(primary school TA)*

If you are an experienced assistant changing your role, the same will apply. A clear job description (see Appendix A) will go some way to clarify your role and a good induction course or further training will help too. Thirty years ago, assistants were mainly employed as welfare assistants to do a lot of 'housekeeping' tasks such as 'washing out paint pots and clearing up messes', to quote from one job description. This seems hardly believable now. With an increase in the attention on supporting children and young people with special educational needs in the 1980s, the role changed to one of learning support, and since then it has continued to develop into a wide range of roles and responsibilities. One focus is common to all roles, and that is the promotion and support of learning, social inclusion and well-being of children and young people. How best to do this is addressed later in this book.

> 'When I started 15 years ago, I was just a pair of helping hands. Now I have to know much more.'
>
> *(infant school TA)*

Possible roles

When TAs are asked to define their supporting role, their responses fall into four main categories:

- supporting the pupil;
- supporting the teacher;
- supporting the curriculum;
- supporting the school.

These different aspects of support are explored in detail in Chapters 3–6.

In infant, junior or primary schools, or in early years settings, you could be employed to give:

- general in-class support to the teacher and the children;
- specific support for a group of children who have identified special educational needs, including learning and/or social, emotional and mental health difficulties;
- specific support for an individual child with significant learning needs;
- tailored support for an individual child with a medical need;
- support for the delivery of a particular learning programme;
- language support for children whose first language is not English;
- a combination of the above.

In secondary schools you could be employed to give:

- general support to a curriculum area (e.g. English, maths, science);
- support to a group of students with learning and/or social, emotional and mental health difficulties;
- support to individual students who have additional learning, behavioural or medical needs;
- delivery of specific programmes (e.g. for literacy or numeracy), including assessing progress;
- lesson cover (if you have a Higher Level Teaching Assistant qualification);
- support for students whose first language is not English;
- a combination of the above.

In special schools or special units you could be employed to give:

- general classroom support;
- support to individual children who have very significant special needs;
- delivery of specific programmes (e.g. speech therapy or physiotherapy);
- support with self-help needs (e.g. feeding, changing, toileting);
- support for inclusion in a mainstream school;
- a combination of the above.

What are my responsibilities?

This is one of the first questions you will be asking. The answer does of course depend on your particular role. In your work as a TA you will be working as part of a team; in a secondary school this is usually the learning support team in the school which is led by the special needs coordinator (SENCO), who will make clear to you your responsibilities and which pupils you will be working with. It may be that you will work mainly in one classroom and with one teacher, for example in primary and early years settings. In this case your work will be managed by the teacher and supported where appropriate by the SENCO. The majority of teachers really value the work of the TAs they work with.

'I could not run the class without the support of my TA. We are a team, we know what we are doing and we work together to help the children make progress.'

(early years teacher)

When we talk of learning support this usually refers to additional help over and above what most children and young people need. In its widest sense, all teachers give learning support to all pupils and certainly all class teachers have the responsibility for the learning programmes of all pupils in their classes, whatever their learning needs.

In an infant school, particularly in the early years, you will work very closely with the teachers as part of the year group team, giving general support to the children and specific help to those who need it. In junior schools you are likely to be part of the year group team, working closely with the teachers and supported by the SENCO who will give advice about additional educational needs and individual learning programmes (ILPs)/individual education plans (IEPs). In a secondary school your responsibilities will usually be directed by the SENCO or by the head of department in the curriculum area in which you work. Sometimes you may be managed by a Head of Year (HOY) or a senior teacher responsible for inclusion and pastoral support. Your responsibilities will be mainly directed by the teacher you work with.

It is important for you to remember that TAs are not teachers and should never be overburdened in terms of responsibilities. The class teacher has the responsibility for the education of all pupils in his or her class and the head teacher has the responsibility for all the pupils in the school.

Which pupils might I be asked to support?

In a recent survey of TAs, it is clear from the results that there is an increased emphasis on supporting the learning and progress of *all* pupils. It is also clear that many TAs continue to work with children and young people who are disadvantaged, vulnerable or have special educational needs. The term 'vulnerable' covers a range of different groups which you may be asked to work with. The Ofsted guidance 'Evaluating Educational Inclusion' (2005) has the following list:

- looked after children
- children unable to attend school due to medical needs
- traveller children
- asylum seekers and refugees
- young carers
- school refusers
- teenage parents
- young offenders.

The National Foundation for Educational Research (NFER) identifies socially vulnerable children as those:

- living in vulnerable accommodation
- at risk of sexual exploitation

● at risk of drug use
● from low-income families
● from families where there is domestic abuse or substance abuse
● from families where there is breakdown or change in circumstances.

Only a small minority of TAs work directly with pupils identified as gifted and talented (G&T), although you may work with such pupils in group work activities.

If you are working with any pupils who need additional support arrangements, the class teacher has the responsibility to ensure that appropriate programmes are planned, followed and monitored. These will usually be detailed on the pupil's individual plan, e.g. an ILP or IEP or in group work programmes. Some secondary schools call these individual plans 'student learning profiles' (SLPs). If the pupil has a behaviour problem then the programme may be called an individual behaviour plan (IBP) or a pastoral support programme (PSP). As an assistant, you are expected to work under the guidance of the class teacher to meet the needs of the child or young person. There may be occasions when you are expected to work on your own with one or more pupils. In these situations you need to work as a responsible adult and do your best to ensure the well-being of each pupil.

In specific curriculum lessons there will be particular routines to follow, e.g. when supporting a pupil in food technology or in science practical lessons you may need to have an appropriate health and safety qualification. There will be a member of staff in your school who is responsible for health and safety and who can give you advice about this. There are guidelines, e.g. for staff who accompany pupils off-site and for staff who may be involved in administering drugs to children. Your SENCO should be able to direct you to any information needed.

What if something goes wrong?

Every employee of the local authority is covered by a general employment insurance policy held by that authority. By law, you are deemed 'a responsible adult' and the duties performed by you are delegated to you by the head teacher. If something does go wrong, you should discuss the situation with the teacher who is responsible for your work and with the head teacher also. In the case of any accident, it must be recorded in the schools' incident/accident book. In the case of injury to a child, your first priority is to see that the child is given first aid and that the class teacher is informed. Safeguarding children and young people has, quite rightly, become an issue of great importance over the past decade and it is vital that you understand your role and responsibilities in relation to safeguarding and child protection (see 'Safeguarding' in Chapter 6, 'Supporting the school').

What support can I expect?

It is sometimes the case that TAs are 'thrown in at the deep end' with no clear idea of what is expected of them.

'I felt in at the deep end although other TAs were very supportive.'

(junior school TA)

'It's O.K. Off you go – you'll be all right'

If you are not clear about what you are expected to do, then you do need to ask. Confusion can be prevented by:

- a clear job description (see Appendix A for an example);
- communication between the class teacher/SENCO and the assistant so that you are clear about
  - the ground rules for working with the teacher;
  - the expectation of how you will work in the lesson;
  - any individual learning plans.

What might I be asked to do?

The role of the teaching assistant will vary from school to school, and also within schools, depending on the school's organisation and on the needs of individual pupils, or groups of pupils. It is important that you know what your duties are from the start in relation to different pupils. You need to know whether you are working mainly with one individual or are expected to work with small groups, or sometimes with the whole class.

In an audit of TA tasks, described in the book *Maximising the Impact of Teaching Assistants* (Russell, Webster and Blachford 2013), The main categories of tasks are described as follows:

Support for teachers/curriculum, e.g.

- classroom preparation;
- worksheet preparation;

- IEP and lesson plan development;
- preparation and maintenance of resources and equipment;
- record keeping;
- support and use ICT.

Direct learning support for teachers, e.g.

- deliver lessons covering teacher absence (higher level teaching assistant: HLTA);
- deliver learning activities;
- deliver interventions/booster programmes;
- give feedback to pupils;
- perform pupil assessments (e.g. reading tests);
- provide specialist pupil support;
- reward pupil achievement;
- supervise pupils out of class;
- support excluded pupils;
- help pupils to understand instructions and achieve learning goals.

Direct pastoral support for pupils, e.g.

- attend to pupils' personal needs;
- develop one-to-one mentoring;
- administer first aid/welfare duties;
- help pupils make choices;
- support behaviour management programmes;
- provide guidance and advice.

Indirect support for pupils, e.g.

- interaction with parents/carers;
- monitor and record pupil progress.

Support for school, e.g.

- admin tasks;
- telephone duties;
- liaison/meetings with external agencies;
- support attendance/pastoral systems;
- record keeping;
- support and use ICT;
- assist with health and safety;
- re-arrange classrooms and school areas including displays.

Specific tasks

You may not be asked to do some of the tasks above but you are very likely to undertake tasks related to pupil learning. Some of the more usual tasks assistants are asked to do are as follows:

- explaining teaching points and repeating instructions given by the teacher;
- delivering or supervising learning programmes, (e.g. for literacy or numeracy);
- working in class with a small group to follow up the main lesson points;
- producing worksheets and resources for the pupil, in consultation with the teacher;
- reading stories to children on an individual or small group basis or hearing them read;
- playing a learning game with a pupil or small group;
- making notes for the pupil as the teacher is speaking which can be used in the work that follows;
- checking the work pupils produce and helping them to correct their own mistakes;
- acting as a scribe;
- helping younger pupils change for PE (or older pupils who have physical disabilities);
- explaining words the pupil does not understand, encouraging use of dictionaries;
- guiding computer-assisted learning programmes;
- using a Dictaphone for recording information – you may need to transcribe what the pupil dictates;
- reading textbook sections or questions to the pupil;
- supervising practical work;
- helping the pupil catch up on missed work or homework;
- observing a pupil's way of managing a task – only intervening if the pupil cannot do it independently;
- keeping the pupil and others 'on task';
- reporting back to the teacher, especially problems or successes;
- contributing to planning and review meetings about the pupil;
- helping children learn their spellings.

What are the ground rules?

These are guidelines for you to use in working with a particular teacher. They should be discussed with teachers before you start work as a TA or, for experienced assistants, when working with a new teaching colleague.

Teachers will have their own ideas and you need to ask about these before you start so that you can reduce confusion and provide a consistent approach. Also, you need to know what authority you have when working in the classroom. The more you understand the workings of the class and the way the teacher operates, the easier it will be for you to work within the class and to support the pupils who need help. Here are some suggestions of questions to ask in order to determine 'ground rules':

1 How shall I be introduced to the class?

It is important that you are, in fact, introduced to the class at the beginning of the school year so that pupils know who you are and what your role is. It is also important that you are introduced in the right way so that the pupils' perception of your role is clear. Discuss this with the class teacher.

An introduction such as: 'This is Mrs Smith and she is Andrew's special helper' is probably not helpful, both in terms of Andrew being pointed out as 'special' and of raising the idea of Mrs Smith as some kind of 'minder'. A more useful introduction might be: 'This is Mrs Smith who will be working with me to help you all to do your best. Sometimes she will work with one or two of you and sometimes with small groups.'

2 How do I work with other pupils?

Even though you may be responsible for only one or two pupils, the others will note your presence in the classroom and ask you for help. You should be prepared to tell them something about yourself and, as far as possible, treat all pupils in the class in generally the same way, giving help to them as well as to the pupils assigned to you if they ask for it. You should encourage them to accept the pupils you work with as a full members of the class.

3 Can I give pupils 'permission'?

E.g. When a child asks to go to the toilet, can I give permission?

It is likely that children will ask your permission on frequent occasions about how to act in certain situations. Discuss this with the teacher so that you know what to do.

4 Can I 'mark' books?

E.g. When a pupil comes to show me some written work, when is it appropriate for me to mark their work?

It is likely that this will be acceptable for you to do when working individually or in small groups with children but, generally, the teacher will need to do this. However, it has become increasingly the case that teachers welcome TAs correcting some aspects of a pupil's work, e.g. spelling mistakes or using a ruler correctly. Again, check with the teacher about how best to help and read the school's marking policy.

5 Where shall I sit in the classroom?

E.g. When is it appropriate for me to sit right by the pupil and when should I stay at a distance?

This will depend on the particular activity and you will learn, with practice, when it is necessary to give individual support and when to withdraw and allow the pupil some independence. Observing how the pupil works from a distance can give you important clues about their ability to manage tasks. It is really important not to 'stick like Velcro' to pupils as they may become too dependent on you. This can be an unintended consequence of providing extra support to individual pupils and will not support the pupil in becoming an independent learner. You will see this point raised in later chapters as it is a trap into which many assistants fall.

6 What shall I do if I see some misbehaviour?

E.g. When two pupils are 'winding each other up', shall I intervene and, if so, what sort of approach should I use?

There are bound to be occasions when you see things going on of which the teacher is unaware. You need to negotiate with the class teacher how you should react to such situations and know when it is appropriate to refer the situation to the class teacher rather than deal with it yourself. A quiet and assertive direction to the pupil such as 'Get on with your work' is often enough to stop the behaviour or even just a 'look' is sufficient to show them that you have noticed. You should familiarise yourself with the school's behaviour policy and follow the guidance there. Pupils in most schools are well behaved, but if you see a physical fight then you will need to act. The school will have a restraint policy as part of the behaviour management procedures and you will need to read that so you know what to do. There are recommended ways of managing such incidents.

7 Can I contribute or ask questions during the lesson?

There may be times when you feel you can add particular information which will add to a class discussion. The teacher may sometimes ask for your view. You may also feel the need to ask for clarification – possibly for yourself or, more often, if you can see that the pupil is not clear. TAs have many skills, so if you can add to lessons from your own knowledge or experience, do let the teacher know as most do welcome contributions. However, do avoid becoming the 'overgrown pupil' in the classroom (described by M. Balshaw in her book, *Help in the Classroom*).

8 What is the best use of my time?

You need to negotiate a timetable which is able to use your support to best effect. You also need to agree with the teacher when your presence is needed and when it might be of more use for you to be doing some small group work or preparing materials for the pupil or pupils you support, e.g. Should I sit in on school assemblies when I am not really needed? Sometimes in lessons you may feel that your time would be best used in another way. Always consider the purpose of your presence/intervention in terms of benefits to the pupils you are supporting. Discuss this with the teacher, making positive suggestions about how you could contribute. In other words, become proactive rather than reactive. TAs, especially in secondary schools, report that they sometimes feel wasted in the lesson so need to be more proactive in managing their time. Speak to the SENCO if this is the case.

'As TAs we need to learn to manage our own time and be more creative with the time we've got.'

(secondary TA)

9 Will I be expected to talk to parents?

You may well be seen as an extra source of information by parents who approach you at the school gate, in the playground, or even at the supermarket. They may want to know about their own child's progress, complain about other children's behaviour, or even criticise the class teacher. It is important at times like this to be professional and not collude with the parent or jeopardise your relationships with colleagues. Practise a way of being polite but firm, e.g. 'I will pass that on to Mrs Smith and ask her to have a word with you'. Confidentiality is such an important issue and you should discuss with the teacher what is for 'sharing' and what is not. TAs in some schools have responsibilities for parent contact or liaison and some run groups for parents and preschool children.

10 Will there be time for planning?

This is, and has been over the last 20 years, such an important but contentious area. Time for planning is always at a premium in school but it is important to know what is going to happen in lessons and how you can be most effective. Joint planning with assistants has become much better in primary schools where teachers and TAs work in closer proximity. Most primary stage TAs report that they see lesson plans in advance so have a good idea about their support role. However, it remains more difficult in secondary schools, where teachers are often moving from lesson to lesson and working with different assistants. Many secondary TAs report that they don't see lesson plans and fewer than half have time for planning and discussion with the teachers they work with. Some secondary schools are now addressing this issue. It is easier for those secondary TAs who work mainly in subject areas, as they are working with a smaller number of teachers on a regular basis and become experienced in the lesson content as it is delivered year on year. For those supporting individual students in many subject areas, it is more problematic.

'It works best when you have the same TA in each lesson.'

(secondary maths teacher)

If possible, you need to find time for planning so that you can discuss the pupils you will be working with and how you will support them. Ask for copies of lesson plans or schemes of work so that you can check in advance what role the teacher wants you to play in the lesson or suggest how your time and skills could best be used. Again, become proactive rather than reactive in your role ... ask questions ... make suggestions ... most teachers will be glad to hear your views.

'TAs should ask for help if they are not sure.'

(secondary teacher)

What do TAs enjoy about the role?

A survey of 8,000 TAs by the trade union UNISON was carried out in 2013 (UNISON, 2013). This included TAs from all types of schools. The survey revealed high levels of job satisfaction amongst TAs, with 95 per cent believing their job makes a difference to the lives of others. It is clear that the majority of TAs get a lot of job satisfaction from helping pupils to succeed. Here are some quotes from that survey:

> 'I love my job and the satisfaction I get from helping a child to learn something new.'

> 'The workload seems a lot at times but the rewards are amazing.'

> 'To see a child succeed at something you have helped them with is the most amazing feeling.'

> 'I enjoy making a difference to students and the way they feel when they come to school.'

All TAs report that teamwork is important to their job satisfaction and the great majority work in supportive teams.

> 'I enjoy being part of an experienced and supportive team.'

What do TAs find difficult about the role?

Working with pupils

The issues raised by TAs working with pupils are mainly related to the increased academic pressures they perceive.

> 'There are now more pressures of targets on teachers and children.'

> 'Putting students through GCSEs when it is just too difficult for them to manage, even with allocated hours of support.'

There is now more recording of information and some TAs feel that this gets in the way of working with the pupils.

> 'There is more paperwork, form filling, testing. This takes me away from my time with the children.'

Working with teachers

Although the great majority of TAs report good relationships with teachers, there are a few whose experience with a minority of teachers is not enjoyable.

> 'Being in a class when a teacher couldn't care less if you are there and sometimes fails to acknowledge you at all.' (NB In the majority of lessons, teachers do work well with assistants.)

> 'Being expected to be the behaviour support when children with needs have to go unhelped because you are supporting behaviour.' (NB In the majority of lessons, teachers manage the behaviour of pupils well.)

Pay and conditions

In the Unison survey, 95 per cent of TAs reported concerns about low pay. In 2013, 87 per cent of TAs were on term-time only contracts and some contracts were temporary. This leads to a lack of job security and a view that the job is not given the professional status it requires.

'We need to be more recognised as a profession.'

Three-quarters of TAs expressed concern about the lack of suitable and affordable training and professional development opportunities (see also Chapter 13) and a similar percentage had concerns about an increased workload and working unpaid hours.

'There is not enough time, I am sometimes very rushed.'

'The job and its expectations has changed a lot over the years but it is still enjoyable.'

How has the role changed over recent years?

The essential role of the TA in giving good support to teachers to help them teach and to learners to help them learn has not changed, but there have been three significant changes in education that have had an impact on the work of TAs. These are:

- the increasing focus on raising standards;
- the impact of computer-assisted learning and the internet;
- the inclusion of children and young people in mainstream schools who have a greater diversity of need.

The increasing focus on raising standards in schools

Assistants need to be more aware and informed about their role in promoting effective learning (see Chapter 7).

'There is now the pressure of targets placed on the children and teachers (and so us).'

'The job requires much more skill and ability to assess children's progress.'

Research from the Education Endowment Foundation (2015) found that TAs can provide 'noticeable improvements' to academic achievement when they are delivering structured interventions, either in small groups or one-to-one. It also shows that TAs help to ease teacher workload and stress, reduce classroom disruption and allow teachers more time to teach, which has an indirect positive impact on achievement. TAs also play a vital role in pastoral support for pupils, enabling them to cope with the demands of school life.

'The differences I make are to children's health, well-being, safety and happiness; this enables them to attain.'

(from Unison survey)

The impact of computer assisted learning and the internet

Information and communication technology (ICT) has developed a lot over the last 20 years. Nearly everyone has mobile phones and many use the internet and email. Computers, word processors, iPads and tablets are now used routinely in schools and at home to support learning and pupils use the internet for communication and gathering information. Social networking sites such as Instagram, Snapchat and Facebook are widely used by children and young people.

There are differences in the ways that schools use ICT, with good schools using it routinely in lessons to support learning. Children and young people in our schools have grown up in a culture that is more and more influenced by technology. Most pupils enjoy lessons in how to use computers and many children and young people know more than their TAs or teachers! ICT is developing all the time as devices become more sophisticated and, in your role as a TA, you need to become confident in using ICT because it is so widely used in school.

> 'The use of ICT has changed; we need to have technical skills in using tablets and iPads.'
>
> (junior school TA)

If you don't feel confident in your ICT skills, there is usually a teacher or a technician in the school who will be able to help you learn the skills you need. There are often local courses in Adult Education Centres that you can attend. One issue you need to be particularly aware of is e-safety. We hear stories in the news of cyber-bullying, where pupils send messages on mobile phones that cause distress to others. We also hear of children and young people being targeted by adults for harm on social media websites. As part of your safeguarding duties (see Chapter 6, 'Supporting the school') you need to report anything you see or hear of which may harm the pupil.

The greater diversity of special educational needs

Over the last 20 years mainstream schools have admitted many pupils who might previously have been educated in special schools; this is called *inclusion*. TAs report that there is now an even greater diversity of additional needs presented by children in mainstream schools. This means they have to know something about these needs and the different ways of working with children who have very different backgrounds, abilities and personalities. Many assistants state that flexibility is a key quality necessary to do the job.

> 'We have to cope with a much greater diversity of need so we have to be adaptable and flexible people!'

In addition, TAs report that there is an increasing number of children and young people who show more stress at school. They think this is because there is more pressure on children to achieve academic success and also because of increasing family breakdown. TAs note that they have an important nurturing role, e.g. checking the child has had breakfast, helping with uniforms and equipment and reassuring students about examinations.

They recognise that it can be easy to become drawn into family issues and to worry about individual pupils but that it is important to keep a professional distance.

> *'We have to have emotional resilience and not get too involved with children's family problems.'*

Inclusion

The 1981 Education Act states that:

> 'Where possible, all children with special educational needs should be educated in ordinary schools.'

and

> 'For integration to be effective, pupils with special needs must be engaged in all or most of the activities of the school. Some pupils with special educational needs require *extra help* if they are to benefit from the experiences available to all pupils.'

TAs often provide this 'extra help', which makes it possible for children to attend ordinary schools. Since the 1981 Act, many children who might previously have been educated in special schools have been educated in ordinary (i.e. mainstream) schools. The majority of these children require various different educational arrangements for some of the time in order to make the best use of the opportunities offered to them in mainstream schools.

What is meant by inclusion?

We now refer to 'inclusion' rather than 'integration'. This philosophy was first referred to in *Excellence for all Children* (DfEE October 1997) and is now part of school culture. A useful definition was provided in an Ofsted report from 2000 called 'Evaluating Educational Inclusion'.

> *'Educational inclusion is more than a concern about any one group of pupils such as those pupils who have been or are likely to be excluded from school. It is about equal opportunities for all pupils, whatever their age, gender, ethnicity, attainment and background. It pays particular attention to the provision made for the achievement of different groups of pupils within a school.'*

Inclusive education means that all pupils, whatever their learning support needs, learn together in age-appropriate classes in local schools. Staffing and resources are made available to all, according to their needs, so that every child can participate in the life of the school. Rather than individual children proving their readiness for integration, inclusion means that the school must be ready, willing and enabled to accept all children, so it is a whole-school philosophy.

As a result, we now have many more children and young people in mainstream schools who were previously educated in special schools.

'Two pupils from special schools are attending the mainstream primary full-time with support. All achieved with TAs' commitment.'

(from Unison survey)

These are mainly pupils with mild to moderate learning difficulties, although many schools cater for a wider range of needs, including autistic spectrum disorders (ASDs), physical disabilities, hearing or visual impairment and severe learning difficulties, e.g. Down's syndrome. TAs are really important in enabling children with significant needs to be included successfully in their local schools.

'I supported two children with Down's syndrome over four years. Pupil support assistants play a big part in primary education.'

(from Unison survey)

Some mainstream schools have special units which have staffing and resources so that pupils with quite significant needs can avail of the support they need in their local schools, e.g. units for hearing/visual impairment, physical disability or ASD. TAs linked to these units play a valuable role in supporting the inclusion of pupils with this kind of need in some or all mainstream lessons. There is still a need for special schools for children and young people whose needs are too complex to be met in mainstream schools. TAs in these settings provide particular support for care and welfare needs as well as learning support. Whatever the type of school, it is key that all staff work together to enable the child to have a successful learning experience and to be a participator in their local community.

Schools sometimes feel unable to support disabled children yet children with and without disabilities have much in common. If 'learning support' based on individual and group needs is put at the heart of school development planning and the school aims to tackle the full range of needs, then this can improve the learning environment for everybody. When we think of learning in this way, the proposals for moving some children in special schools into local mainstream schools can be realised, given the right levels of support.

'It is evident that every child will gain from an inclusive approach. All children can feel comfortable and supported as an inclusive approach recognises [that] every one of us has a variety of abilities. Growing up as friends with people who may look or sound very different means losing fears and unfamiliarity which turn into prejudice. The inclusive approach will lead to children developing into adults who are able to accept and value difference.'

(Rieser 1994)

In your work as an assistant it is important that you are aware of the wider perceptions people in society have about children who are viewed as different and that you work to encourage an understanding and acceptance of difference as part of everyday life.

'They wouldn't give us these labels if they had to wear them afterwards'

Activity

Think about your current role as a TA and how you might be more proactive.

- Is there anything you could do more of?
- Is there anything you could do less of?
- Are there any changes you could suggest to the teacher/ SENCO?
  e.g.
  Use of your time?
  Access to lesson planning?
- What do you need to do to develop your role?
  e.g.
  training
  working with other TAs

CHAPTER 2

How to be an effective teaching assistant

Chapter summary

- What makes an effective teaching assistant?
- How can I be effective in lessons?
- How can I be effective working one-to-one?
- How can I be effective in running groups?
- What does research say about my effectiveness?
- What qualities do I need to be effective?
- What advice would experienced TAs give to someone starting the job?
- Activity

What makes an effective teaching assistant?

In a nutshell, an effective TA is someone who:

- enables pupils to make good progress in their learning;
- fosters the self-esteem, social inclusion and well-being of pupils;
- works confidently and sensitively with teachers to promote learning;
- has the necessary interpersonal skills to relate well to others.

In 2015, a Department of Education working group identified four helpful themes to guide the effective working of teaching assistants. These are:

- personal and professional conduct;
- knowledge and understanding;
- teaching and learning;
- working with others.

Personal and professional conduct

A school is a public workplace so, as a TA, you need to act professionally following school policies and procedures. To provide effective support to teachers and pupils, you need to be clear about your role and responsibilities and how these fit within the wider structure of the school (see Chapters 1 and 6). In the same way as teachers, teaching assistants operate in a position of trust and are seen by pupils as role models. As a TA, you have a responsible position and so you should maintain proper boundaries with pupils, parents/carers and school staff, being friendly and supportive but not getting too involved in personal or family issues or sharing confidential information.

You should seek to develop good relationships with the school community by demonstrating a positive attitude and a 'can do' approach to school life. As an effective supporting professional, you need to be able to review your own work and be willing to improve your knowledge, skills or understanding of any aspect of your role.

Knowledge and understanding

To work effectively as a TA, you need to know what you have to do and how to do it. You need the knowledge and skills to help teachers support pupils in achieving their maximum potential. School managers and SENCOs are best placed to make judgements about the type and level of knowledge and skills that individual teaching assistants need, as this will vary according to the job role. This could include: subject knowledge, specialist skills and knowledge to support pupils with special educational needs or disabilities, knowledge of the curriculum, lesson planning and evaluation, and behaviour management strategies (see Chapters 9 and 10).

Teaching and learning

A really important aspect of effectiveness is supporting the teacher in ensuring the best possible outcomes for all pupils (see Chapter 7). Teaching assistants need to watch good teachers in action so that they can learn the strategies and approaches which promote effective learning. Particular ways of working may be needed for pupils who have special educational needs. A very important aspect of this is promoting independent learning so the pupil does not become dependent on you, as discussed in Chapter 1. You will also need to learn effective ways of encouraging good learning behaviour and managing disruptive behaviour (see Chapters 9 and 10). You need to promote social and educational inclusion by encouraging pupils to value each other and to participate in school activities.

Working with others

Teaching assistants work with other professionals, parents, carers and outside agencies as well as with pupils. To be effective in this area, you need to learn the skills of communicating relevant, accurate information, reporting back verbally or in writing and using your initiative to make useful contributions. If you have any concerns about pupil progress or well-being, you need to alert the teacher you normally work with. Working effectively in partnership with outside agencies and parents means being aware of their perspectives and skills and respecting their views.

How can I be effective in lessons?

Your effectiveness in lessons depends quite a lot on the skills of the teacher and on how well he or she deploys you.

'I would like to be more directed by the teacher as to who they want me to work with and how they want me to approach it.'

(secondary TA)

You need to be clear about what the pupils are expected to learn by the end of the lesson. It will be an important part of your job to find out how best to work with each pupil, according to their needs, and how much to expect of them – not too much, and not too little. Remember that you should be helping them to learn 'on their own' – weaning them off support if at all possible – so beware of making them too dependent on you. Doing the work for the pupil is a big temptation and a big trap that many assistants fall into! Don't do it! (You will find this point emphasised throughout this book.)

"Yes — well done Mrs Smith, you got 10/10 for those sums!"

Every lesson will have a lesson plan, either a specific plan for an individual lesson or a medium-term plan which details the content of a group of themed lessons.

If you can see a copy of the lesson plan before the lesson then it will help a lot with your effectiveness as you will know what is coming up. Most plans specify which pupils need additional support and the best plans indicate what the role of the TA will be in the lesson. Teachers do not have 'eyes in the back of their heads', so they often value what you see and hear from your perspective as part of the lesson. All the research points to the value of joint planning with teachers but it still remains difficult to do this in some schools, especially secondary schools. There never seems to be enough time but, where time is made for joint planning, the learning outcomes for pupils are improved.

To be an effective TA in a lesson you need to know

Before the lesson:

- The learning objectives or outcomes of the lesson and its place in the curriculum.
- What you should do and when you should do it.
- Which pupils may need additional support.
- What behaviour management strategies the teacher wants you to use.
- Whether you need to prepare any materials or worksheets.
- Whether you will be needed to work with a small group or individual pupil.
- Whether you can mark books during the lesson.
- What assessment you may need to do.

During the lesson:

- Be aware of the learning objectives throughout the lesson.
- Use differentiated materials or worksheets.
- Observe how pupils get on with the task.
- Give individual support when needed.
- Work with a group of pupils.
- Work flexibly if the teacher changes the plan.
- Keep students 'on track' by directing them back to work.
- Take notes as requested.

After the lesson you need to:

- Feedback to the teacher what worked well and what did not work well with the pupils you were with.
- Provide any written notes if you have taken any.
- Consider whether any changes are needed for the next lesson.

How can I be effective working one-to-one?

Working one-to-one sounds easy but it can be tricky if the pupil is not motivated, is reluctant to be singled out or is unhappy about being moved away from the group. Some pupils love it but others don't, especially older pupils who are more sensitive about being treated differently. To be effective you need first of all to establish a good relationship with the pupil. Before getting into the task, some social chat about interests or school life is always helpful. Working one-to-one provides a great opportunity for interaction, so taking turns, e.g. in a reading task, is a helpful strategy.

> *'A girl joined Year 1 unable to read or write. After daily sessions she has become a confident reader who enjoys books.'*
>
> (infant school TA)

Sometimes pupils lose interest in the task so you need to notice when this is happening and change the activity or liven it up in some way. If the activity is not working it may be too hard, too easy, or just boring so do not persevere with it and change it if you can. If you find yourself with a stroppy teenager who has been excluded from the class, you will need all your powers of negotiation and problem-solving to settle them down. You will need to consult with the teacher about what to do if there are difficulties.

How can I be effective in running groups?

Research shows that TAs can be really effective in helping pupils improve their literacy and numeracy skills by running structured groups. Some TAs support social skills or anger management group work. You will need training if asked to lead such groups.

> *'I've led early morning and after school booster maths lessons. There's been significant progress in the children.'*
>
> *(from Unison survey)*

Group work provides opportunities for greater pupil interaction and closer observation of what each child can do. It also provides pupils with good opportunities for social chat and off-task behaviour. Managing groups is not always easy. However, if you want to be effective, then follow these tried and tested guidelines:

- Set the ground rules for group work with the pupils where possible and make them clear (e.g. we take turns and don't all talk at once). This establishes routines.
- Seat pupils away from others who might distract them.
- Give clear assertive instructions.
- Be well prepared and make a brisk start to activities.
- Praise the group at an early stage for getting down to work.
- Give time reminders.
- Use visual or auditory aids if possible.
- Use your acting skills, using your voice and non-verbal actions to engage the pupils.
- Make plenty of encouraging comments and praise pupils by name for making good efforts.
- Record outcomes to report back to the teacher.

Most pupils like group work as they get more attention and can often see that they are improving.

> *'Pupil feedback has been positive. They say "I learn better in a small group" and "I couldn't have done it without you".'*
>
> *(from Unison survey)*

What does research say about my effectiveness?

There have been a number of studies on the impact of assistants. Some of the findings are interesting and have significant implications for head teachers, special needs coordinators (SENCOs) and teachers in the way assistance is used and managed (see Chapter 11). As an assistant, you are to some extent 'a hostage to fortune' as your everyday work will be very much influenced by the teachers you work with, and you will be limited in what you can do to change this. However, it is important that you are aware of recent research findings as you may be able to work more effectively to enable pupils to make better progress.

A guidance report called 'Making Best Use of Teaching Assistants' (Education Endowment Foundation) was published in 2015. Some key recommendations from this report are issues which school management teams need to address. However, there are some findings which TAs can take on board to improve their effectiveness. These are as follows:

> 'TAs tend to be more concerned with task completion and less concerned with developing understanding.'

In observing TAs at work, the researchers noted that some TAs tend to close down talk and 'spoon-feed' answers. Over time this can limit understanding and pupil thinking skills. To be effective, a TA needs to learn the skills of effective questioning (see Chapter 7) and not be too concerned if the task is not finished. More important is the learning process, allowing the pupil time to process the information and understand the ideas being taught. Some pupils learn at a slower pace than do others so it can be very tempting to do the work for them, but this is counter-productive.

> 'TA support may increase dependency.'

This is because some TAs tend to think for the pupil rather than allowing them time to think for themselves. Over-reliance on one-to-one TA support is not good in terms of responsibility for learning and separation from classmates. A degree of sensitivity is required here. There are times when one-to-one is helpful but it is important that it is not overused. Pupils can quickly get used to someone else doing the work.

> 'TAs help ease the teacher's workload and stress, reduce classroom disruption and allow teachers more time to teach.'

Teachers are mostly positive about the contribution of TAs in classrooms, reporting that increased attention and support for learning for those pupils who struggle most has a direct impact on their learning. Helping with organisational tasks helps to ease teacher workload.

> 'Use TAs to deliver high-quality, one-to-one and small-group support using structured interventions.'

The research indicates that TAs are very effective in improving learning when they are used to deliver specific programmes, e.g. Accelerated reader, Catch Up programmes, Phono-Graphix, Reading Recovery, First Class at Number. TAs report that they enjoy delivering these interventions as they are clear about what they are doing and can see the impact they make on pupil progress.

> *'My maths intervention work with a group of low ability Year 2 pupils raised attainment by several levels over two terms.'*
>
> *(from Unison survey)*

What makes an effective TA? The teachers' view

Secondary teachers report that they have support from assistants in over half of all lessons. All say that the support helps students to learn with over half reporting that it helps a lot.

> *'I need the TA to respond to pupil needs, be consistent in expectations of behaviour, to have authority and react calmly.'*
>
> *(secondary teacher)*

> *'TAs must ask when they are not sure.'*
>
> *(secondary teacher)*

Most support time in lessons is a combination of general support and that given to students who have special educational needs or those who have pupil premium funding (additional funding for pupils who may be disadvantaged). Three-quarters of secondary teachers had no specific training in how to make best use of assistance although the same proportion would welcome such training. Nearly all teachers said that there is not enough time to plan together with assistants.

In lessons, the main thing that teachers want is for assistants to be proactive rather than reactive. Secondly, they want them to understand how children learn. Good literacy and numeracy skills are also seen as valuable. The main piece of advice that teachers would give to someone starting out as a TA would be to research the learning needs of the student. Half report that joint planning is a key aspect of the partnership working and a third think that clarity of roles is important. However, over half do not give written lesson plans or schemes of work to assistants.

Teachers in early years settings and primary schools have support from assistants in most lessons. Just as for secondary teachers, their advice to TAs is to ask questions, to ask for support if they need it and to observe experienced staff. More primary TAs see lesson plans in advance and this helps them to be effective in lessons.

What makes an effective TA? The SENCOs' view

SENCOs say that the job has changed over recent years and that more is now expected of assistants. Academic qualifications are now asked for by many schools, particularly GCSE qualifications in English and maths as the focus is more on supporting learning in addition to the pastoral role that TAs have traditionally undertaken. TAs have a wider range of responsibilities than previously, including leading group work, running mentoring sessions and taking responsibilities on school trips. SENCOs report that it has become harder to find the right people and that applicants are some-times students who want to go into teaching or trained teachers who do not want the full responsibility of a teacher's role. SENCOs also report that it is still difficult for assistants to get the training they need because of local access difficulties and funding shortages. However, when TAs get specific training, e.g. in autism, they are more effective. It remains the case that much TA time is spent supporting children and young people who have some kind of learning difficulty or behaviour problem. In secondary schools, some TAs are assigned to curriculum areas, particularly English, maths and science. This improves their effectiveness as they get used to working with a smaller number of teachers and become familiar with the curriculum.

The following qualities were described by a group of teaching assistants:

- patience
- care
- sense of fairness
- consistency
- sensitivity
- ability to learn from mistakes
- flexibility
- versatility/adaptability
- positive attitudes
- friendliness
- being hard to shock/thick-skinned
- sense of humour
- enthusiasm
- calmness.

Most TAs possess many of these qualities and become aware of areas which need to be worked on.

What qualities do I need to be effective?

'Saint or superwoman? – or both!'

1 Ask questions

When asked what advice they would give many assistants emphasized the importance of asking questions.

'Always ask questions even if you feel you should know as sometimes teachers expect you to know without explaining things!'

2 Be flexible

Being willing to change and adapt to pupil needs, teacher needs and lesson requirements was another key point.

'You just have to go with the flow and be prepared for anything. I try to follow how each teacher works and how they manage behaviour, etc.'

'Be flexible, smile and don't get too stressed or too involved with students and take things personally.'

3 Develop good channels of communication

Communication with teachers is clearly important and this means establishing good working relationships. You can do this by asking questions and having a positive and supportive attitude.

'Try to talk to the teacher so you are clear about what is happening in the classroom.'

4 Don't worry about making mistakes

Making mistakes is a key part of any new learning experience. Everyone does it and as long as you learn from it and move on, it is what happens. Of course, you must share with the teacher if anything has gone really wrong and most teachers will be supportive.

'Don't worry when things go wrong and don't take students' failure personally if you have done your best.'

5 Learn from other TAs and teachers

You will find that other TAs will be only too happy to help you. Watching good teachers at work will also provide good role models.

'Shadow an experienced TA and ask for advice.'

'Be patient, listen, don't judge a situation on first appearances.'

6 Take every opportunity to develop yourself

There will be opportunities to improve your knowledge, skills and understanding through reading, through watching others, through in-school training and through external courses.

'Read, go on courses. Share ideas with colleagues.'

7 Use your initiative and be as proactive as possible

Teachers welcome TAs who intervene sensitively and don't need too much direction by the teacher. This comes with experience of course. It is much easier to use your initiative when you are used to the teacher and familiar with the lesson content. It is harder if it is a 'one–off' lesson or working with a supply teacher, particularly in secondary schools.

'You need an awareness of what needs to be done and the initiative to get on and do it.'

8 Make learning fun

Many TAs have an upbeat and positive attitude towards teachers and pupils and this helps enormously in making the school an enjoyable place to work. A sense of humour goes a long way to enjoying learning experiences and diffusing difficult situations.

'If an activity is enjoyable, it will be more successful.'

(*junior school TA*)

Activity

How to be an effective teaching assistant

Consider how effective you are.

- How could you be more effective in lessons?
- How could you be more effective working one-to-one?
- How could you be more effective in running groups?
- What qualities do you already have?
- What qualities do you need to be more effective?
- What advice would you give to someone starting the job?

Supporting the pupil

Chapter summary

– Which pupils will I be asked to support?

    – Special educational needs

    – Medical needs

    – The pupil premium

    – First language not English

– How can I support individual pupils?

    – Aspects of the support role with pupils

    – Supporting pupils who have literacy difficulties

    – Encouraging reading

    – What is paired reading?

    – Encouraging spelling

    – Supporting pupils who have numeracy difficulties

– Activity

Which pupils will I be asked to support?

This depends on the role you have negotiated with the teacher. It could be that you are there to give general assistance in a lesson, in which case you will work with any pupil or group of pupils as directed by the teacher, or as you see the need. Many teaching assistants (TAs) are asked to work with groups of pupils and some with individual pupils. Even if you are giving general support to a curriculum area, the pupils you are most likely to work with and who will need additional support will fall into the following categories:

● They have identified special educational needs.

● They have identified medical needs.

● They are entitled to the Pupil Premium (additional funding for disadvantaged pupils).

● They have short-term needs (e.g. pupils whose first language is not English).

Special educational needs

There is a continuum of special educational needs (SEN) ranging from mild short-term difficulties with learning to profound and multiple learning difficulties, which require long-term support into adulthood (see Chapter 9 for more details). TAs support the progress and well-being of children and young people with SEN in a wide variety of ways, both pastoral and academic.

Medical needs

These pupils learn in a normal way but have specific medical needs, e.g. children with muscular dystrophy, cystic fibrosis, epilepsy, etc. (see Chapter 9).

TAs provide practical help for this group of children (e.g. ensuring that they have the right equipment, following physiotherapy routines, etc.) They may need help with catching up if school work is missed for health appointments or hospital visits.

The pupil premium

This is additional funding given to schools to support the education of children and young people who are disadvantaged (e.g. Looked After Children [LAC] – children 'in care'), pupils eligible for free school meals (15.2 per cent, DfE statistics 2015), Young Carers (e.g. who have a parent at home who is disabled), and children of service personnel who move around a lot. Some of the funding is spent on providing experiences (e.g. school outings, sports clubs, equipment or musical instruments).

Often the funding is used for additional literacy or numeracy support and TAs are deployed in many schools to give this sort of support. These pupils may or may not have special educational needs. Generally, the progress of pupils identified as needing the Pupil Premium is not as good as that of other pupils. The additional funding is there for schools to use to accelerate the progress of this group and 'narrow the gap' between their achievements and the achievements of 'non-pupil premium' pupils.

First language not English (English as an Additional Language, EAL)

There is an increasing number of pupils in our schools whose first language is not English. Department for Education statistics (2015b) indicate that 15 per cent of pupils in secondary schools and 19.4 per cent in primary schools come from homes where English is not the first language. This is particularly the case in big cities and other areas of the country where some secondary schools identify more than 40 languages other than English being spoken at home. While the majority of these children will not have any special educational needs and some may be proficient in English when they join the school, some assistance will be necessary if they come from abroad or have not mixed with English speakers. Some local authorities provide EAL assistants who are bilingual so that they can help pupils to settle in and learn the basics.

How can I support individual pupils?

Whether you are supporting specific pupils or not, you will need to:

- Ensure you know which pupils in the class need some kind of support.

- Ensure that you interact with these pupils during the lesson.

- Pay attention to their progress, encourage their engagement and their efforts.

- Be proactive in supporting learning, for example, getting them to correct spelling errors or checking that they understand what they have to do.

- Use prepared, differentiated activities and report back on their effectiveness.

- Discuss any concerns about progress or behaviour with the teacher.

Aspects of the support role with pupils

TAs identify the following aspects of their supportive role with pupils:

- promoting independence;
- promoting progress;
- inspiring confidence and trust;
- valuing the pupil;
- fostering peer group acceptance;
- encouraging and giving rewards;
- developing listening skills;
- enabling the pupil;
- knowing the background;
- finding out about any learning support needs;
- keeping confidences;
- being 'in tune' with the pupil's physical needs.

Promoting independence

This is an absolutely key concept in your role. You are there to give varied levels of support depending on pupil needs but, for *all* of the pupils you work with, you must at all times be seeking to encourage them to attempt new tasks without your support and to work independently whenever possible. It is common for TAs to feel that they must always be 'one step ahead' but, in fact, the idea of being 'one step behind' is much more helpful in promoting the independence of the pupil. If you are always foreseeing pitfalls and removing them from the path of the pupil, then he or she will never learn strategies for coping in the real world. You have to let them 'have a go' before you step in.

However, there will be times when you will have to act in order to pre-empt serious situations – common sense is a necessary quality!

Some assistants feel that if they are employed to work with one particular pupil, then it is appropriate to 'stick like glue' to that pupil … this has been called the 'Velcro' model, as mentioned in Chapter 1. Though there are times when the pupil will need individual support, it will often be appropriate to help the pupil within a small group or even to spend time standing back and observing the behaviour of the pupil in classroom situations. You may be surprised at how much he or she is capable of. You will be doing the pupil no favours if you encourage their dependence on you. In fact, you should be aiming to be so effective in promoting the independence of the pupil that you work yourself out of a job!

Your role is not to do the task for the pupil

Promoting progress

This has become an increasingly important role of the TA. All pupils make progress in their learning as they move through school, apart from the very small minority who have degenerative medical conditions. Just as there is a range of shoe sizes in the population, there is a range of learning abilities, linked to a number of factors, including intelligence, environment, expectations, confidence and motivation. Some children start school and seem to learn to read and make good progress without needing very much tuition. Often they have nurturing homes which provide a lot of support. Other children struggle to cope with the demands of school and this is where TAs can provide valuable additional adult attention and support, thus enabling the young child to settle into school and start to learn. It becomes very clear to the school at an early stage which children are going to require additional support in order to become effective learners. As they move through the primary stage and on to secondary education, some pupils will no longer need additional TA help but others will continue to need support until they leave school. Those with severe and complex learning needs will require continuing support beyond their school years and into adulthood. This support for learning includes help in the classroom and sometimes follows specific learning programmes under the guidance of the class teacher, e.g. computer programmes, commercial packages or schemes recommended by the local authority or Department for Education. (See Chapter 7, 'Promoting effective learning'.)

Inspiring confidence and trust

Often it is the case that pupils, particularly those with special educational needs, are lacking in confidence. Children become aware of failure very quickly and they lose confidence when they see their classmates making progress while they struggle. Pupils who have had difficult social histories may feel that they have been 'let down' by the important adults in their lives and feel it is hard to trust someone to be consistent, fair and encouraging. A pupil with a low opinion of himself or herself, for whatever reason, is going to begin to expect to fail. It is, therefore, vital that you take every opportunity to point out what the pupil is good at and to lead them to expect that they can succeed. Think out ways of providing frequent opportunities for real success. It may take time but if you have a consistent, positive and fair attitude towards the child, he or she will learn to develop confidence and to trust you. Praising effort on the way to a finished piece of work can work really well.

Valuing the child

No child can learn effectively when they are not feeling valued. It is a key role of an assistant to value the child. Any pupil who is thought of

Wow!

as 'different' from other pupils may encounter negative attitudes, particularly if the disability is obvious. Surviving childhood teasing is often dependent on self-esteem, so it is very important that the pupil feels secure and highly regarded by the important people in his or her life, and you are one of them. Valuing includes behaviours such as greeting the pupil by name, showing interest in their interests and encouraging their progress.

Fostering peer group acceptance

Any child wants to feel that they *belong* to a group; indeed it is part of human nature to want to belong. It is part of your role to encourage the other pupils to value any pupil or pupils who might be excluded by social groups. This entails drawing attention to those skills the pupil is good at, or to some particular achievement. It may also involve valuing the contributions of the pupil, e.g. making him or her group leader in appropriate activities. Some children need help to improve social skills, i.e. the way they relate to others. If the pupils you work with have poor social skills then you can help them by practising appropriate responses first in play-acting, then in real situations. For younger children it might be helpful to act out a well-known fairy tale, e.g. Billy Goats Gruff, with each child being able to take on different roles. This can help children explore feelings and relationships – the troll seen as a 'bully' and the little billy goat Gruff seen as the 'victim'. This sort of activity can lead to discussions about feelings and rights and wrongs. For older pupils, discussing real situations and then role-playing to consider the best outcomes can be extremely helpful.

Encouraging and giving rewards

Giving the pupil encouragement and praise is a *very* important part of your role and will contribute in a large part to the development of self-esteem and confidence. Liberal amounts of encouragement and praise must be given. *Meaningful* praise means telling the pupil why you are pleased with him or her, e.g. it is better to say 'Gemma, I like the way you have used colour in this picture' rather than 'That's a good picture', or 'Tom, you listened to the story well today' rather than just 'Good boy'. Some studies have shown that praising the effort a pupil has made has more impact than general praise, e.g. 'Jake, I am really impressed by the effort you have made'. 'Sarah, you have really tried hard with that writing'.

Praise and encouragement is all you will need for most pupils and the good thing is that it is easy to give it once you have developed the habit … you always carry it with you! Some pupils may need more tangible rewards. All pupils respond to rewards if the rewards are motivating and achievable. You will need to find out what might work. Here are some ideas you could suggest as incentives, but remember to ask the pupil first what they would like as a reward once they have achieved what you have negotiated.

Ideas for rewards

Primary age pupils

- extra 'choosing time', when he or she can choose an activity;
- extra time on the computer;
- a favourite game;
- a bubble-blowing session;
- making biscuits, cakes or sweets;
- stickers to wear and keep;
- decorating plain biscuits with icing and 'sprinkles';
- doing an 'important' job for the class teacher or head teacher;
- music while you work;
- letter or certificate sent home to parents.

Secondary age students

- extra time on the computer;
- letter or certificate sent home to parents;
- position of responsibility;
- a special interest project;
- free ticket to school disco.

It is important to ensure that the reward is achievable over a short period of time to start with, so that success is encouraged. For younger children particularly, the reward needs to be earned within one day so that it is immediate. Other children may be able to work towards a reward at the end of two or three days, or at the end of a week. Again, you will need to negotiate this with the class teacher so that there is consistency in your approach.

Developing listening skills

When you start working with a pupil, it is tempting to do a lot of the talking and to expect that the pupil has taken in what you have said. Remember that effective communication is a two-way process and that some pupils need time to get their thoughts together and to express themselves. Some are only able to understand short bits of information at a time. You may need to check that the pupil has understood you by asking him or her to repeat back to you the information you have given or that the teacher has given to the class. This simple technique is called 'perception checking' and is an extremely valuable skill to practise and use regularly.

Pupils with emotional difficulties can be helped enormously by someone providing a 'listening ear'. This means that when the pupil is talking, you give him or her your full attention and are able to make encouraging gestures such as nodding and smiling. Non-verbal 'messages' from you to the child are, in fact, more important than the words you use.

You can learn to encourage pupils to talk by choosing the right phrases. This is called Active Listening. Brenda Mallon, in her book *An Introduction to Counselling for Special Educational Needs,* gives the following helpful examples:

Listening skills

Types	Purpose	Examples
Warmth, support	To help the pupil.	'I'd like to help you; are you able to tell me about what is the matter?'
Clarification	To get the complete 'story' from the pupil.	'Can you tell me more about it?' 'Do you mean.........?'
Restatement	To check our meaning is the same as the pupil's.	'From what you are saying, I understand that...................'
Encouragement	To encourage the pupil.	'I realise this is difficult for you but you are doing really well.'
Reflective	To act as a mirror so the pupil can see what is being communicated. To help pupils evaluate their feelings. To show you understand the feelings behind the words.	'You feel that.........' 'It was very hard for you to accept...........' 'You felt angry and upset when...........' 'I can see you are feeling upset...........'
Summarising	To bring together the points raised.	'These are the main things you have told me...................' As I see it, your main worry seems to be...................'

If you are able to use some of these skills then you will be well on the way to being a good listener and, more than that, you will help the pupil to work through whatever is causing worry or concern.

Enabling the pupil

The pupil who needs support with learning often feels unable to attempt tasks which other pupils have no problem with. As we have noted already, your role is not to do the task for the pupil but to enable the pupil to do that task for himself or herself by providing the necessary 'tools for the job'. This may mean:

● explaining the task clearly when the pupil has not understood (if the problem persists, see the teacher);

- making sure the pupil knows what equipment is necessary, where it is kept and how to use it;

- helping the pupil to organise his/her thoughts and consider how to set out the work;

- encouraging the pupil to arrive at the lesson on time and with the correct equipment;

- giving the pupil strategies to use to help him/her remember information, e.g. writing lists, keeping a diary;

- working with small groups to encourage sharing and cooperation.

You may need to adapt the worksheet provided by the teacher so that the pupil can understand and do the task; this is a really helpful activity, both for the pupil and the teacher. Making a task simpler in this way is called *differentiation* and it is done so that the pupil is more likely to understand and learn.

Knowing the background

The individual pupil record will provide some information about the child's background and you can ask the teacher if you want to see it. You will understand the pupil's difficulties better if you know something about the pupil's home life and the way he or she spends time out of school. This is about valuing the pupil too.

It will help you in establishing a relationship if you find out early on who the other family members are, whether the pupil has any pets and what hobbies or special interests he or she has. You may find it valuable,

Show an interest in the child's interests ...

particularly with younger children, to keep a scrapbook entitled 'All About Me', into which you can put photographs and snippets of written information about what happens in the life of the child. The child will feel valued when you show interest in the things which are meaningful to him or her. For the older child this can also be a useful activity. Writing an autobiography, e.g. 'My Life Story', can be particularly helpful to pupils who have emotional difficulties and low self-esteem.

Finding out about the learning support needs

It is the responsibility of the class teacher or the special needs co-ordinator in the school to ensure that you know what you need to know about the pupil's particular needs in order to do the job successfully. If you feel you don't know, do ask. There is likely to be a list of pupils with special educational needs in the school together with individual learning programmes or behaviour plans. There is also a network of services external to the school, e.g. speech and language therapists, physiotherapists, teacher advisers, educational psychologists and child psychiatrists who can be approached, together with your class teacher, should you want to find out more information. There are also many charitable organisations which offer information about a wide range of disabilities, e.g. SCOPE (formerly the Spastics Society) and the Royal National Institute for the Blind. (Appendix B provides more information about the roles of supporting professionals.)

The information contained in the pupil's school records will give you some background knowledge. You will need to check with the head teacher whether you can have access to this information (see Chapter 9, 'Supporting children and young people with special educational needs').

Keeping confidences

This follows on well from the last point. When you work closely with a child or young person, there are bound to be times when you hear or see information, e.g. about the home life, which must be kept confidential. This does not apply, however, to disclosure of child abuse, which is information you have a duty to share with the head teacher (see Chapter 6, 'Safeguarding'). In the course of your job, you may find people confiding in you. While you can discuss information with other professionals concerned, please remember that the information you come across in the course of your job is *not* for discussion or comment with outsiders. (See Chapter 1 for more on confidentiality.)

Being 'in tune' with the pupil's physical needs

This refers to the physical well-being of the pupil. There are occasions when a child comes to school feeling tired, hungry or just not well. This is particularly the case with pupils who have physical disabilities and who may have had disturbed sleep. Children from non-nurturing homes are also at risk. When working with such children and young people, the session is not always likely to be an academic success. Don't feel you have failed if nothing is achieved on paper sometimes – quite often showing a genuine interest in the pupil and lending a sympathetic ear goes a long way towards compensating for what may be lacking in his or her background. Be aware of any moodiness or lethargy and make allowances for it. Imagine how you feel yourself when you are tired or run-down, and treat the child with gentleness and sensitivity. There is growing evidence that poor diet can influence energy levels and concentration so, as part of your nurturing role, you may be able to give advice about healthy eating. Some schools have breakfast clubs where pupils can get something nutritious at the start of the school day. When working with secondary age students you may need to be alert to signs of drug taking or alcohol mis-use and be prepared to report anything suspicious to the teaching staff if you are concerned.

Supporting pupils who have literacy difficulties

Some pupils find difficulty in developing literacy skills, and this is the most common difficulty you will meet in school. In your work as an assistant you are sure to come across these pupils and you will need to know how best to give support. TAs have a really important role to play in supporting pupils who need help to develop reading, writing and spelling skills. The *Primary National Strategy* report, 'Teaching assistants in Year 6 (DfES 0340-2004'), showed the positive impact on attainment in schools that had trained TAs to work with targeted children in Year 6. Research shows that TAs can be very effective in delivering specific programmes to support pupils who find literacy difficult.

> *'Children punch the air and shout "yes" when they are called to come and do Catch-Up literacy with me'*
>
> *(from Unison survey)*

There are a number of literacy learning programmes which you can be trained to use, e.g. Reading Recovery, Accelerated Reader, and Phono-Graphix, and it is clear that TAs enjoy this aspect of their work.

Trained TAs can work with the teacher to ensure all pupils experience quality teaching in English lessons and also in other lessons which require literacy skills. This will involve working with the whole class, groups and individuals. All schools teach English as part of the national curriculum and in primary schools English is part of the daily timetable. This often includes whole-class work, sharing a big book or a shared passage, whole-class sessions on words or sentences, small-group work on directed activities and often there is a short session at the end for reporting back and planning.

Your role in English lessons will be planned by the teacher you work with but is likely to include:

- preparing resources and setting out tables;

- encouraging pupils to look and listen;

- demonstrating how to do the task;

- supporting discussion;

- asking questions to assess learning;

- modifying activities so the pupil can understand the task;

- observing and assessing how the pupils are managing;

- sitting close to pupils who find it hard to concentrate;

- clarifying or repeating instructions or tasks;

- working with a group on activities planned by the teacher;

- reporting back to the teacher if the pupil is experiencing difficulties.

Encouraging reading

When sharing a book with a child do remember:

- An encouraging manner is vital to success.

- Some pupils have poor memories so activities designed to develop memory skills are important.

- Use techniques which encourage success, e.g. you read most of a sentence leaving some words to be read by the child.

- If a child gets a word wrong NEVER say 'no'. Correct by saying: 'This word is ... Can you say it now?'

- Allow some mistakes if this does not stop the general flow of reading.

- Make it fun for younger children by hiding a page that has just been read and asking quiz questions about the meaning or the pictures.

What is paired reading?

Paired reading is when an adult or another more proficient reader reads aloud at the same time as the child. This method is excellent for parents, grandparents, carers and assistants to encourage reading and is ideal for books that are rather too difficult for the child to read alone. The child is encouraged to follow the text and to read simultaneously with the skilled reader. In reality, the reader is likely to lag behind fractionally so it is important to adjust the pace so the child can keep up. (You may need to slow down!)

As the child develops confidence he or she is encouraged to indicate, usually by a small gesture, if he or she wants to try reading on their own. The skilled reader then stops reading until signalled to join in again or the child begins to struggle. This method has been found to be very successful in developing children's reading skills and boosting their confidence. It takes away some of the stress often involved in reading practice where there can be too much emphasis on accuracy. It also enables pupils with reading difficulties to read books that are of particular interest to them. You can adapt this method to suit the child. You may start reading a sentence and the child finishes the sentence, reading alternate lines or paragraphs. Do whatever works best.

Encouraging spelling

Many teachers use simple techniques of LOOK/ COVER/ WRITE/ CHECK to help children to learn spellings. This is just as it sounds:

LOOK	The child looks at the word – saying it aloud will also help as will tracing over the letter shapes with a finger.
COVER	The word is covered up.
WRITE	The child tries to write the word from memory.
CHECK	The child checks whether the word is right and tries again if not.

There are many software programmes which help children to improve spelling skills which are used in good schools and the spellchecker facility on word processors is very useful.

Encouraging writing

Many pupils are disheartened when it comes to putting pen to paper because it is difficult for them. When helping the pupil do remember:

- Encourage any effort the pupil makes on his or her own.
- Check that the pupil is sitting and holding the pen correctly. There are pencils which help with hand grip. Pupils who are left-handed will need help as they write so that they do not cover their work.
- Some pupils find it difficult to copy from the board. You may need to transcribe work onto paper for copying.
- Some pupils find it easier to record work using a word processor, especially those who find it hard to write neatly. Do encourage this whenever possible as it is often more motivating for them, especially as it is not judgemental so they can 'fail' without anyone seeing!

There are a number of programmes which encourage writing such as THRASS, which supports spelling and writing (www.thrass.co.uk).

Supporting pupils who have numeracy difficulties

Some pupils, often those with special educational needs, require additional support to develop numeracy skills – the skills of understanding concepts of size, shape, relationships and number. Many find it difficult to do mental arithmetic or simple computation tasks. In all schools, maths is a key part of the curriculum and in primary schools it is taught every day.

This includes regular exercises in mental arithmetic, problem-solving and teaching of new skills. Whole-class work and small-group support are part of these lessons. There are additional programmes to support children and young people who struggle with numeracy, e.g. 'First Class at Number.' TAs often deliver these programmes and, as with literacy programmes, are very effective in doing so.

> *'My maths intervention work with a group of low ability Year 2 pupils raised attainment by several levels over two terms.'*
>
> *(from Unison survey)*

> *'The schools maths results went up by 12 per cent last year because of small-group intervention.'*
>
> *(Unison survey)*

Encouraging numeracy

When working with a pupil who has numeracy difficulties do remember:

- The basic language of maths needs to be taught and understood.
- The pupil needs to learn concepts of size, shape and classification as basic building blocks to understanding.
- Learning using practical apparatus and equipment is necessary for many pupils, particularly in the early years.
- Pupils who have poor memory skills will need lots of practice and repetition.

There are a number of good software programmes now available which children find attractive and that help them to learn.

Additional information can be found as follows:

- Fox and Halliwell (2000) *Supporting Literacy and Numeracy* and Halliwell *Supporting Special Educational Needs* (2003) offer more advice on giving support (David Fulton Publishers).
- The Assessment for Learning unit in *Excellence and Enjoyment: Learning and Teaching in the Primary Years* (DfES 0518-2004 G).

Activity

Think about one or more of the pupils you often work with.

- How do you promote their independence?
- Are they too dependent on you?
- Do you ever do the work for them?

- What do you do which shows the pupil that you are interested in them?
- How to you encourage pupils to accept and work with each other?
- Are you clear about the learning support needs?
- Is there more you need to know about supporting literacy and numeracy?

CHAPTER 4

Supporting the teacher

Chapter summary

- Three key themes
  - Inclusion
  - Achievement
  - Independence
- What do teachers say about assistants?
- How can I support the teacher?
  - Working in partnership
  - Preparing classrooms and resources
  - Supporting the delivery of the lesson
  - Giving feedback about how the pupil manages the work
  - Helping to set targets, monitor and evaluate programmes
  - Recording information
  - Keeping pupils 'on-task'
  - Spotting early signs of disruptive behaviour
  - Modelling good practice
  - Freeing up the teacher to work with groups
  - Maintaining a sense of humour
- Activity

Teaching assistants (TAs) work with teachers to:

- foster the participation of all pupils in the social and academic processes of a school or setting; [INCLUSION]
- help raise standards of achievement for all pupils; [ACHIEVEMENT]
- encourage independent learning; [INDEPENDENCE]

(quote from The Management, Role and Training of Learning Support Assistants: Department for Education and Employment 1997)

So, as an assistant working with a teacher or teachers, you need to have these three key themes in your mind at all times. All are discussed in the previous chapters.

What do teachers say about assistants?

It is clear that most teachers really value their TAs.

> *'They are worth their weight in gold!'*

> *'My TA keeps me sane! The job would be impossible without her.'*

How can I support the teacher?

TAs identified the following aspects of their supportive role with respect to the class teacher:

- working in partnership;
- preparing classrooms and resources;
- supporting the delivery of the lesson;
- giving feedback about the how the pupil manages the work;
- helping in setting targets, monitoring and evaluating individual learning programmes;
- recording information;
- keeping pupils 'on-task';
- spotting early signs of disruptive behaviour;
- modelling good practice;
- freeing up the teacher to work with groups;
- maintaining a sense of humour.

Working in partnership

Working in any partnership implies *communication*. In order to work well with a class teacher you must feel able to ask questions, clarify expectations and get feedback on your work with the pupil. It is a two-way process and obviously much depends on the personality and organisational skills of the teacher, on whom you are dependent for direction and guidance.

However, if you are to work effectively it is vital that you meet regularly for information exchange, joint planning and evaluation. In a primary school it need only be for a short time each day or each week but it is in the best interests of the pupils that you do this. In a secondary school this is more difficult as you may be supporting the pupil in up to ten curriculum areas. You may find it more practical to have one longer planning session per month. Planning does take some time commitment by the teacher but you will be better able to support him or her if you are both clear about what you are both doing (see Chapter 12 for more on planning).

To quote from the Audit Commission/HMI *Handbook* (1992a): 'Where extra help is provided, planning and communication are the keys to improving its impact.' This document also stresses the need for the supporting adult to 'be aware of the class teacher's objectives for a piece of work so that he or she can then focus on what the child is to master, and consider alternative means of reaching the same goal.'

Working in partnership can be a problem, particularly for TAs working in secondary schools who will have to work with a number of different teachers. Some staff may have subject specialisms and it may be necessary for you to ensure that a member of staff understands the way in which you can assist a pupil in a given situation and the limitations of that pupil.

A small minority of teachers feel threatened by the presence of another adult in the classroom. If you feel uncomfortable about any situation it may help to discuss your concerns with the special needs coordinator and the teacher concerned. But do remember that your main role is not to give 'marks out of ten' for the quality of any lesson or any teaching style, but to act in the best interests of the pupils whom you are employed to support and enable them to make the best of any teaching situation.

Preparing classrooms and resources

Teachers really value the help they get from TAs in preparing for lessons and activities as it frees up teaching time and reduces stress levels. Most TAs, especially those working at the primary stages, will spend some time each day sorting out equipment, worksheets and workbooks for use by the pupils and assisting with the class layout to support the lesson. Small tasks, such as ensuring pencils are sharpened, can save valuable lesson time. As a TA, you may be involved in creating new resources and learning games for pupils to use. TAs who deliver small-group interventions are able to prepare the resources they need for these programmes. In a secondary school practical lesson, you may be asked to help in setting up science apparatus or getting materials ready for an art or textiles lesson.

Supporting the delivery of the lesson

We have looked at how to be effective in lessons in the previous chapter as it is such an important part of your role. A TA who has been briefed about the lesson objectives and content is in a good position to support the teacher. A close partnership that works to deliver the learning outcomes is key to improving pupil achievement. One factor that teachers identify as very helpful is proactive rather than reactive assistance … this, of course, depends on how well the teacher has briefed the TA. When observing lessons, it is clear to see whether the assistant is proactive or reactive. If you go into any early years lessons it is often very hard to tell who the teacher is and who the TA is as they work so closely together. Part of your role in supporting the delivery of the lesson is to ensure that pupils follow the teacher's directions and do as well as they can in completing the work set. When you notice that pupils are not coping with the task it is usually because they think it is too hard. They might not have understood the directions or the teaching point. Sometimes they cannot read the language on the worksheet or the layout is not sufficiently engaging. When you see this happening, you will need to 'differentiate' the task. This means adapting it in some way to make it understandable for the pupil. One real example of this was observed in a secondary school geography lesson in which the assistant could see that a few students were struggling to understand the worksheet. She used her initiative to simplify the worksheet by making amendments to it, picking out the key words and making some of the writing bigger. This made it easier for the students to understand.

Giving feedback about how the pupil manages the work

Feedback about how well the task is managed is such a valuable part of any learning process and TAs often do this informally, catching a few minutes at the end of a lesson to report back to the teacher on the progress of pupils who may have had some difficulties. As in the previous point, it is sometimes the case that tasks are too hard or presented in such a way that the pupil does not 'get it' and so learning is ineffective. The assistant can often see this happening and can step in to help and can report back to the teacher so that the task can be modified or presented in such a way so that it is accessible by the pupil. In working closely with a particular pupil or group of pupils, it is likely that you will be more sensitive to their needs and reactions in any given situation than the teacher, who takes a wider view. You will be able, therefore, to provide information to the teacher about how well the pupil is coping with the demands made on him or her. This may involve written feedback or record keeping. If a task given to the pupil is too difficult, please don't feel you must persevere with it to the bitter end, but instead feed back to the teacher that this is the case and either get the teacher to modify the task or agree that you yourself can do this. Teaching assistants are often wonderfully creative given the opportunity, so feel confident in making suggestions and modifications as you feel necessary. The majority of teachers will be only too pleased to hear your ideas and take them on board if possible.

Some schools have devised simple feedback forms which can be used by the assistants to give helpful feedback on assessment of progress. One example is as follows:

TA Lesson Feedback

Date _____

Name of Pupil _____

Lesson _____

On a scale of 1–5 how did the pupil perform? (1 is low, 5 is high)

On task?	1 2 3 4 5
Understood lesson content?	1 2 3 4 5
Good behaviour?	1 2 3 4 5
Followed teacher directions?	1 2 3 4 5
Co-operated with others?	1 2 3 4 5
Completed set work?	1 2 3 4 5
Dependence on TA support?	1 2 3 4 5

What worked well?

What did not go well?

Any ideas to help the pupil learn more effectively?

In addition to feedback about how the pupil is coping with school work you will also be able to provide information about the general well-being of the pupil and about situations out of school or in the playground which may be affecting the pupil's performance in class.

There are some TAs who support the teacher by undertaking literacy assessments, e.g. using reading tests to measure pupils' reading ages. Training in how to do testing is necessary for this kind of task. Feedback from such activities provides very useful information for teachers and TAs.

Helping to set targets, monitor and evaluate programmes

In an ideal situation, when you are meeting regularly with the class teacher or special needs coordinator, you will be able to make a contribution to the planning of individual programmes. It is the responsibility of the class teacher, with the support of the special needs coordinator, to do this for each pupil with special needs, as they will decide what the next step is for the pupil. You will be able to contribute ideas about how this might be done, bearing in mind your understanding of the pupil's work and his or her temperament. Each plan will have set targets which you will need to work towards. If you feel that some targets are too easy, or too hard, then you need to say so.

"And I'm hoping that he'll have cracked long division of decimals by the end of next week."

It is also extremely valuable to *evaluate* what you are doing with the pupil. This means 'taking a step back' periodically, say every half term, or even more frequently, and asking yourself just how effective your work with the pupil has been and whether the targets or goals set have been achieved. If not, or only partially, it would be worth discussing alternative approaches with the class teacher in order to see if this makes a difference.

But do remember that many pupils who need learning support often only learn slowly and so realistic expectations are clearly needed.

Recording information

As part of your work in supporting the teacher, it is essential that you record what you do in the course of your work with the pupils. The teacher or special needs coordinator will be able to advise you about the sort of records you should keep and the format this should take. The information you will be asked to record will depend on the particular needs of the pupil. For instance, you may be asked to record details about the language the child uses or about how many times he or she shows aggressive behaviour. Whatever the record is, it should contain useful information to help in planning future work rather than just a diary of events. So it might, therefore, be useful to record the date, the activity and the materials used, bearing in mind why you are doing the task. It would then be useful to record an evaluative comment about how well the pupil succeeded in the task. In any record, it is very important to record successes as well as difficulties. Feeding back success to the teacher will improve the motivation of the child.

Consider:

- Has the pupil learned?
- If not, why not? (task too hard, wrong time of day, too many distractions, unmotivating materials, etc.)
- How might this be done better next time? (Discuss with teacher.)

Keeping pupils 'on-task'

Most pupils find it hard to concentrate for the whole of a lesson … in fact many adults find their minds wandering from a task or listening activity from time to time. However, most lessons require pupils to be on-task for most of the time if they are to make good progress. As a TA, you will often see off-task behaviour, which may range from daydreaming to social chat, and you will need to act to get the pupil back on track quickly. You should remind the pupil of the teacher's instructions and give a positive prompt to get on with the task. A minority of pupils may need some 'time out' because of attention or sensory difficulties and this should be part of their learning programmes.

Spotting early signs of disruptive behaviour

As a TA, you are an extra pair of eyes and you will often see behaviours which the teacher has not noticed. It is very helpful to the teacher if you can spot any pupil who is starting to distract others, e.g. tapping, rocking on the chair, taking another pupil's equipment etc. You can usually manage this behaviour yourself and there are several alternatives. Moving closer to the pupil and giving a 'look' can be effective, as can removing, without comment, any object causing the problem. As for 'off-task' behaviour, a quiet re-direction to the pupil to get on with their work often helps, particularly if it is followed by a 'Well done!' if the pupil gets back to work.

Modelling good practice

In supporting the teacher, it is good for pupils to see you model what is expected. So, if the teacher is talking, you should be showing good listening behaviour and when activities start, you should be quick to get going with the task. If pupils have not listened to the teacher's instructions, you will sometimes need to model what the teacher has said and demonstrate what is required. Another example of modelling is when a TA reads to a pupil who has English as an additional language, providing a model of good English. A few teachers complain that TAs sometimes talk too loudly to each other when they are addressing the class and this is distracting.

Freeing up the teacher to work with groups

Where the TA is experienced and confident; they can sometimes work with most of the class, e.g. reading a story, thus freeing the teacher to work with a smaller group of pupils who need additional attention. This ensures that slower learners benefit from direct teacher input. This way of working has been identified by researchers as good practice (see 'Making Best Use of Teaching Assistants', Education Endowment Foundation 2015).

Maintaining a sense of humour

When a teacher has a pupil or pupils with difficulties in his or her class it can become hard work as progress may be slow and the level of attention demanded by these pupils is often high. For the health and sanity of the teacher, the pupil and yourself, it is a good thing to smile and joke about situations that invite it. Do not allow situations to become too 'heavy' – having a sense of optimism and good humour can help the teacher and the pupils enormously. Do avoid using sarcasm as this can be damaging to the self-esteem of the pupil.

When the teacher and the TA support each other, it can be of tremendous benefit.

Activity

Enhancing mutual support

Take some time to sit down with the teacher(s) you work with and do the following exercise:

- I am a teaching assistant. How can I best support the teacher? What can I do differently?

- I am a teacher. How can I best support the teaching assistant? What can I do differently?

Supporting the curriculum

Chapter summary

- The national curriculum
  - What is the history of the national curriculum?
  - Why do we need a national curriculum?
  - What are the main changes in the new national curriculum?
  - Which subjects are affected?
  - How is the national curriculum organised?
  - What subjects are included in the national curriculum in England?
  - The curriculum for young children
- How can I support the curriculum?
  - Developing a knowledge of the curriculum
  - Becoming familiar with national initiatives
  - Developing the skills to adapt subject-based activities
- Assessment
  - Methods of assessment
  - How is overall progress assessed in schools?
  - What are schools doing to assess and record progress?
  - Assessment through national tests
  - Implications for teachers
  - What is assessment for learning?
- Activity

As a teaching assistant (TA), it is important for you to know about the national curriculum as this is the basis of all teaching in England.

The national curriculum

What is the history of the national curriculum?

In 1987, the then Education Secretary, Kenneth Baker, announced a statutory (compulsory) national curriculum in England and Wales. It was brought into effect in 1988. A national curriculum was introduced in Northern Ireland in 1992. Scotland has a framework that gives teachers guidance on what should be covered.

Why do we need a national curriculum?

The national curriculum was created because there were concerns over inequalities in what was being offered by schools. The national curriculum set out what children should be taught, with the aim of ensuring that each pupil was given the same standard of education.

A new national curriculum has been taught in all local authority schools in England since the start of the 2014 autumn term.

What are the main changes?

The aim of the new national curriculum is to slim down the content of the curriculum in almost all subjects, though not in primary English, maths or science.

The government says the new curriculum does not tell teachers 'how to teach', but concentrates on 'The essential knowledge and skills every child should have' so that teachers 'have the freedom to shape the curriculum to their pupils' needs'.

The new curriculum covers primary school pupils, aged five to eleven, and secondary schools pupils up to the age of fourteen.

A new curriculum for 15- and 16-year-olds came into force in September 2015.

Which subjects are affected?

There are changes to the content of all subjects in the national curriculum, for example:

- In maths, children are expected to learn more at an earlier age, e.g. to know their 12 times table by the age of nine.
- In the new curriculum, history will take a more chronological approach.
- In English, pupils read and learn more Shakespeare and there is more of an importance placed on spelling.
- The new computing curriculum requires pupils to learn how to write code.
- In science, there is a shift towards hard facts and 'scientific knowledge'.

(*Details can be found on the Department for Education website*: www.gov.uk/government/collections/national-curriculum.)

The five key stages remain the same in the new national curriculum. These are:

- Key Stage 1: Ages five to seven (Years 1–2)
- Key Stage 2: Ages seven to eleven (Years 3–6)
- Key Stage 3: Ages eleven to fourteen (Years 7–9)
- Key Stage 4: Ages fourteen to sixteen (Years 10–11)
- Key Stage 5: Ages sixteen to nineteen (Years 12–13)

The **core** national curriculum subjects are:

- English;
- mathematics;
- science;
- physical education.

The remaining subjects are:

- art and design;
- citizenship;
- design and technology (DT);
- geography;
- history;
- information and communication technology (ICT);
- modern foreign languages (MFL);
- music.

Subjects are compulsory at various stages of pupils' school careers.

For each subject and for each Key Stage, programmes of study set out what pupils should be taught, and attainment targets set out the expected standards of pupils' performance. Schools choose how they organise their school curriculum to include the programmes of study.

The majority of pupils in England follow the national curriculum. Academies (state-funded schools in England outside local authority control) have more freedom in what they teach and do not have to follow the national curriculum.

The 'curriculum' for young children

The early years foundation stage (EYFS) sets standards for the learning, development and care of children from birth to five years of age, using indicators called 'early learning goals'.

All schools and Ofsted-registered early years providers must follow the EYFS, including childminders, preschools, nurseries and school reception classes.

Areas of learning

Children are mostly taught through games and play.

The areas of learning are:

- communication and language;
- physical development;
- personal, social and emotional development;
- literacy;
- mathematics;
- understanding the world;
- expressive arts and design.

Assessments

Progress is reviewed when children are between two and three years by an early years practitioner or health visitor.

Once in school, their class teacher will assess them at the end of the school year when they turn five.

The assessment is based on classroom observation, not testing. It uses the early learning goals, which can be found in the early years framework (www.gov.uk/early-years-foundation-stage).

SEN and the curriculum

All children and young people with special educational needs (SEN) follow the curriculum, although those who have severe and complex needs are often said to be 'working towards' some of the targets set in the curriculum. This is what the Code of Practice 2015 says about the curriculum and SEN:

> '*All pupils should have access to a broad and balanced curriculum. The* National Curriculum Inclusion Statement *states that teachers should set high expectations for every pupil, whatever their prior attainment. Teachers should use appropriate assessment to set targets which are deliberately ambitious. Potential areas of difficulty should be identified and addressed at the outset. Lessons should be planned to address potential areas of difficulty and to remove barriers to pupil achievement. In many cases, such planning will mean that pupils with SEN and disabilities will be able to study the full national curriculum.*'

How can I support the curriculum?

TAs identify the following aspects of their supportive role in respect of the curriculum:

- developing a knowledge of the curriculum which the pupils are expected to follow;
- becoming familiar with national initiatives and their implications for the pupils;
- developing the skills to adapt subject-based activities to meet the needs of the pupils.

Developing knowledge of the curriculum

If you are a TA working in a primary or special school it will be important for you to know about the curriculum and learn about the content of each curriculum area. This will enable you to support the pupils with correct facts and explanations. Over time, you will become more knowledgeable about the curriculum as the same lessons are delivered each year. In secondary schools, more assistants are becoming attached to specific curriculum areas and are becoming very knowledgeable about certain subjects as they learn with the pupils. Assistants report that they like working in this way as they get to know the teachers well and they become familiar with lesson content as it is taught year on year. You may lack confidence at first, but do remember to ask if you are not clear. If you do not understand what is being taught, then it is likely that the pupil does not understand either. Do be aware, however, of becoming an 'overgrown pupil' (see Chapter 1), and know when it is appropriate to contribute, and when it isn't.

Avoid becoming the 'overgrown pupil'

Becoming familiar with national initiatives

The Department for Education has introduced a number of strategies to support the progress of pupils in English schools (see the Department for Education website for details). A significant initiative is the 'Pupil Premium'. The Pupil Premium provides additional funding to schools to help them in raising the attainment of disadvantaged pupils so that they make better progress and catch up with non-disadvantaged pupils. It can be spent on a wide range of things including financial support for school trips and equipment. Most schools use some of the funding to employ TAs to deliver specific literacy and numeracy programmes, e.g. 'Accelerated Reader' or 'First Class at Number' to pupils who may be falling behind as a result of disadvantaged circumstances. Research from the Education Endowment Foundation (2015) shows that TAs can be particularly effective in delivering such programmes.

Developing the skills to adapt subject-based activities

Children do not all learn at the same rate; they have different abilities and aptitudes. In getting to know the pupils you work with, you will become aware of their individual strengths and weaknesses. You will develop a secure knowledge of what they can manage and of how information should be presented so that the pupil becomes a successful learner. You will therefore find it necessary to adapt activities and worksheets for certain pupils; for example, enlarging maps in a geography lesson for a pupil with a visual impairment, or simplifying a written task in an English lesson by providing the first words of each sentence. This is an example of differentiation.

Assessment

Teachers have the responsibility of *assessing the progress* of children and young people as they learn the subjects in the national curriculum. This means that they look at the work their pupils have produced and assess how they perform in lessons. They use their professional judgement to assess how much they have learned and this then informs the next steps for learning. Assessment for learning is a process which goes on informally in every lesson as teachers look at work and ask questions to probe the understanding of their pupils. Teachers also assess progress through marking and through a more formal process called 'work scrutiny', where they take in the workbooks of pupils and judge how well they are doing in achieving the targets set in the national curriculum. Most schools have up to six assessment points in the school year.

Methods of assessment

There are three main methods of assessment that you need to know about:

Formative assessment
This consists of ongoing assessment notes, including in-lesson observations based on clearly defined objectives. This can be used as a planning tool in identifying 'next steps' for learning, e.g. teachers or TAs annotating and amending lesson plans in the light of pupil achievement. Formative assessment also involves timely feedback to the pupil; it may be the teacher, TA or another pupil providing feedback on a pupil's work, either verbally or in writing.

Diagnostic assessment
This provides a detailed picture of performance and identifies areas of difficulty, e.g. diagnostic reading or spelling tests such as 'Alpha Assess' used

in Key Stage 1, the Vernon Spelling Test or the Dyslexia Early Screening Test (DEST,) which helps diagnose early signs of dyslexia at the end of the Early Years Foundation Stage. These are all tools to inform the next steps for learning and they support lesson planning to meet the needs of individual pupils. TAs are often trained to use these diagnostic tests, which can be used to compare a pupil's score with their previous result. Results provide a benchmark for immediate intervention, e.g. the Phono-Graphix Programme, which supports pupils who have been identified as needing extra support in phonics.

Summative assessment

This provides a 'snapshot' of a child's performance at a particular point in time and includes national tests, e.g. GCSEs, end of Key Stage tests or the Year 1 Phonics tests. Summative tests are usually used to assign pupils a score or grade which helps inform teachers about the attainment of their pupils compared to other pupils nationally. From 2016, school tests will reflect the year-group objectives for the new national curriculum. Other summative tests used are norm-referenced (results compared to the average scores of all children on the test) where results are recorded as a standardised score.

Assistants have a valuable role in supporting the teacher in their assessment of pupil progress. This can be done in a number of ways:

- Some TAs are trained to give reading or spelling tests, which are diagnostic and can help in assessing progress over time.

- In lessons, feedback to teachers on how well pupils are learning is very helpful as it is hard for teachers to assess the progress of every pupil in every lesson. This is formative assessment. As an extra pair of eyes, assistants are often able to observe what the teacher might miss.

- Noticing which particular approaches work with particular pupils and how well they respond to different methods is useful knowledge to feedback to give to the teacher. Also if a pupil is struggling with a piece of work and the teacher has not noticed, it is good for the TA to be able to pick up on this and report back. This is also an example of formative assessment.

How is overall progress assessed in schools?

Until September 2014, overall pupil progress was recorded and reported using *Levels*. So it was anticipated that at the end of infant school (Key Stage 1), the majority of pupils would reach a Level 2, at the end of junior school (Key Stage 2), the majority would have reached Level 4. At the end of Year 9, (Key Stage 3), the majority would have reached Level 5.

Since 2014, this system has been removed following the introduction of the new national curriculum. The reason for the change is given by the Department for Education as follows:

> '*As part of our reforms to the national curriculum, the current system of 'levels' used to report children's attainment and progress will be removed from September*

2014 and will not be replaced. By removing levels we will allow teachers greater flexibility in the way that they plan and assess pupils' learning.'

(Information for Schools: Department for Education 2014)

This flexibility means that schools and teachers can develop assessment systems that focus more on the knowledge, skills and understanding pupils have acquired and allows teachers to identify gaps in learning that need to be taught. There is no requirement for schools to assess in any particular way.

What are schools doing to assess and record progress?

Schools now have the freedom to adopt their own approaches to assessment with the expectation that the vast majority of pupils will secure *Age Related Expectations* (ARE) by the end of each school year. Any tracking systems that a school chooses must link to the specific curriculum statements for each year group, or Key Stage in the case of Key Stage 3.

To support this, topics are broken down into separate aspects, based on end-of-year outcomes, which teachers use to make their judgements about pupil progress and attainment. When their learning is assessed as secure and they have 'got it', pupils are then ready to move on.

It is anticipated that around 80–85 per cent of pupils should have reached Age Related Expectations in each subject at the end of each school year. At the end of each year, a small proportion of pupils will be *below* Age Related Expectations and some will be *beyond* or *above* Age Related Expectations. However, the expectation is that the majority of pupils will achieve ARE through high-quality teaching and ongoing assessment that will identify problems and provide corrective or enrichment activities as necessary. At each assessment point, teachers will begin to be able to see the pupils who are 'on track' to achieve ARE and who are not.

The concept of 'mastery' has been introduced. This means that pupils are really very secure in their understanding of facts, ideas and concepts. Mastery learning consists of learning being broken down into discrete, step-by-step units and presented in a logical order. Teachers must therefore consider the pre-skills needed to allow pupils to achieve mastery, e.g. pupils need to be able to make 'teens numbers' from different mathematical equipment and understand place value before they can be expected to add up two 2-digit numbers. A useful analogy is that of learning to drive. At first, you are unsure of what all the pedals do and how they relate to gear changes and driving technique. As driving lessons progress, you practise and practise until you can coordinate hands, feet and brain to drive safely and confidently. At this stage you are secure in your driving technique and are ready to take your test. Once you have passed your test and have been driving for some time, you will be aware that you can drive without really having to think about it … it has become 'second nature'; you may even find that you have been driving whilst thinking of something else! This ability to do a task without thinking about it is an example of 'mastery'. It is anticipated that pupils will achieve mastery in respect of knowledge, skills and understanding of the national curriculum subjects. The concepts of fluency and deeper learning have also been introduced. Fluency is the ability to apply skills learned in one context to another so, for example, learning about tessellation (how shapes fit together) in maths could certainly support learning in design and technology.

Deeper learning is the deliberate decision of the teacher to enrich or deepen a pupil's understanding by providing opportunities to investigate and practise knowledge in unfamiliar contexts. This reinforces the learning and stops it being superficial learning, i.e. something that can easily be forgotten.

In the new assessment arrangements there are new ideas which affect how teachers and assistants might work together. There is more of an emphasis on pupils 'keeping up' rather than 'catching up'. So as well as leading group work to support literacy and numeracy, the TA might need to work with individuals or small groups to reinforce any learning that the teacher thinks is not sufficiently secure. Or, the TA might need to lead the class in an activity while the teacher works with those pupils who have not understood the lesson content.

Assessment through national tests

From 2016, there are new tests at the end of Key Stages 1 and 2. These will no longer assess pupils in terms of levels but will provide a standardised score, comparing the achievement of each pupil to others in the year group.

The new tests are as follows:

- English reading;
- grammar, punctuation and spelling;
- mathematics.

These tests will be based on the national curriculum and will assess the progress of all pupils. They will be used to set standards of achievement and Age Related Expectations.

Implications for teachers

Teachers must demonstrate:

- Skilled use of constant classroom assessment
- Excellent subject knowledge
- Effective deployment of support staff (including TAs)
- Creative use of time and resources
- Quality teaching
- Flexible planning to include both corrective and enrichment
- Feedback marking.

As a TA you are part of the 'effective deployment of support' role and can support the teacher through a range of activities including:

- Contributing to assessment in lessons (formative assessment/assessment for learning).
- Using your initiative to devise and suggest improved ways of learning.
- Using feedback marking, under the guidance of the teacher.
- Carrying out diagnostic assessment.

What is assessment for learning?

Assessment for learning is mainly about ongoing assessment in lessons. The responsibility for this lies with the teacher but, as a TA, you can support this process, which enables pupils to think more about what they are learning and how they are learning. It has the following elements:

Clear learning objectives

Lots of teachers start their lessons by stating and/or writing the learning objectives for the lesson. This helps students to be clear about the lesson content. Some teachers use learning objectives to say what the pupils will have learned by the end of the lesson. As a TA, it is often helpful if you can ask the pupil to repeat to you what the learning objective is as it sometimes 'goes over their heads'!

Share criteria for good work

This is along the lines of 'This is one I prepared earlier'. Showing an example of what is expected by the end of the lesson, and showing other pupils' work which is of good standard can help pupils to know what to aim for.

Make opportunities for self-assessment

This means encouraging the pupil to judge the work they have produced and say whether they are working quickly enough or following the task correctly. It is also a chance for the TA to judge whether the pupil understands the task.

Make opportunities for peer assessment

This means getting another pupil to say whether the work is correct and sufficient. Working in pairs can be very effective as the pupil has to take part and cannot be a 'passenger' in the lesson.

Build confidence, identify and share next learning steps

Stopping for a review mid-lesson can be very helpful in letting the pupil know that they are 'on-track' and can help them to think about what the next step might be. Taking the opportunity to praise effort really helps in building confidence.

Emphasise process, rather than correct answers

If you can help the pupil to think about the task and how to approach it, it will be more of a learning experience than just jumping to the correct answer. As we noted in Chapter 2, one common pitfall that TAs fall into is getting to the end product too quickly and doing some of the work for the pupil.

Use questions well

Questioning is such an important part of learning as it guides the thought processes of children. Think carefully about the questions you ask. Asking a 'closed' question that requires a yes or no answer is not as helpful as asking an 'open' question which requires the pupil to think. Remember the key question words: What? How? Why?

For example:

What makes you think the answer is A rather than B?
How would it be different if you put another adjective in the sentence?
Why do you think that person acted that way in the story? (see also Chapter 7, 'Bloom's Taxonomy')

Encourage 'no hands up' when you ask a question

When working with the whole class or a small group, teachers and TAs often ask pupils to put their hands up to answer questions. If, instead, you ask for 'no hands up', you can ask pupils randomly to answer your questions. This means that they all need to be paying attention as it might be them you choose next!

Activity

Consider how you can support the curriculum.

- How might you develop your knowledge of the curriculum?
- What national initiatives affect your school? What is your role in supporting these? e.g. Pupil Premium?
- How might you adapt materials so pupils can be successful?
- What skills do you need to adapt subject-based activities?
- What is your role in assessment of pupil progress?

CHAPTER 6

Supporting the school

Chapter summary

- School management
  - School governors
  - The senior management team
  - School teams
- How can I support the school?
  - Supporting the school values and ethos
  - Knowing the school policies and procedures
  - By working as part of the learning support, pastoral or curriculum 'team'
  - Working with parents or carers
  - Contributing to reviews
  - Attending relevant in-service training or staff meetings
  - By using particular personal strengths
- Safeguarding
  - What do we mean by safeguarding children?
  - What does this mean for me?
  - What should I be alert to?
- The Prevent duty
- Activity

School management

It will help in your job if you have an understanding of how schools are organised and managed, and how the different teams of staff within schools work.

School governors

Each school has a 'Governing Body' or management board. This is usually a group of about a dozen people who meet regularly to discuss and steer developments in all aspects of the school, e.g. buildings and maintenance, financial planning, staffing, curriculum, pupil progress and head teacher and teacher performance. Although most governors are not teachers, the head teacher will be part of the governing body and there will also be a teacher from the school and at least one parent, ensuring representation from all. You may even consider becoming a governor yourself. You can find out more by looking at the national governors' website (www.nga.org.uk).

The senior management team

Each school has a senior management or leadership team (SMT/SLT). This consists of the head and deputy head teacher(s) and assistant heads in secondary schools. They are responsible for writing the school development plan and managing every aspect of school life, supported by the governors, whom they report to. They appoint new staff and manage appraisal or performance review processes. They also have the responsibility of monitoring teaching and learning in the school so that it is supporting pupil progress. As part of this role, they will also monitor how well TAs are supporting learning.

School teams

In a primary school there are year group teams who meet to plan schemes of work and assess pupil progress by looking at the work that pupils are producing and review any test results. As a TA, you may be included in some of this planning and review, although this is sometimes outside contracted hours. If this is a problem, you will need to speak with your line manager. If your role is to support pupils with special educational needs (SEN) you will work with the special educational needs coordinator (SENCO) and class teachers as part of the learning support team. You can get advice and support about how best to work with the pupils assigned to you. In a secondary school, you will either be part of the learning support team, usually managed by the SENCO, or you will be part of a curriculum team, e.g. in the English or maths department. In fact you may be part of both teams. In secondary schools TAs often support pupils who have social, emotional or behavioural difficulties and in this case you will be part of the pastoral support team in the school, usually led by the heads of year. Sometimes, SENCOs or pastoral support managers are called Inclusion Managers.

Teaching assistants identify the following aspects of their supportive role within the school:

- supporting the school values and ethos;
- knowing the school policies and procedures;
- working as part of the learning support, pastoral or curriculum 'team';

How can I support the school?

63

- working with parents;
- contributing to reviews;
- attending relevant in-service training or staff meetings;
- using particular personal strengths.

Supporting the school values and ethos

Every school has a particular character and, although there are many commonalities, no two schools are the same. The school you work in will have a set of values or principles which underpin its work. You will find these in the school prospectus and often they are displayed in the school entrance. Schools have simplified versions of their values, such as 'Respect, Achieve, Thrive', to quote one example. Make yourself aware of these values and aim to support them as best you can. Most schools will have something about treating pupils and adults with respect and most teacher/TA and pupil/TA relationships are positive and respectful. However, if you find yourself in a professional relationship with either a staff member or a pupil where you find it difficult to be respectful or there is some conflict, you should seek advice from your line manager or the SENCO. It may be that the issue can be resolved or that you need to change the staff or pupils you are working with.

As a responsible adult working in the school, you need to remember that you are a role model, not just for the children but for other adults in the school, and you should try to develop positive relationships with colleagues and pupils wherever you can. Most TAs are very accepting and endlessly adaptable.

> 'You just have to go with the flow and be prepared for anything. I try to follow how each teacher works, as in how they teach, manage behaviour etc.'
>
> (infant school TA)

Knowing the school policies and procedures

You will be able to support the school effectively if you make sure to know about school policies and procedures, e.g. health and safety, accidents and first aid, behaviour management, bullying, SEN, out of school visits, safeguarding (child protection), etc. Ask the head teacher what procedures you need to know about if you are unsure. There will be a big file of school policies available for reference and you need to check which ones are the key policies to support your work. Certainly you should read the safeguarding policy and the behaviour management policies as priorities. If you are supporting a curriculum area, e.g. English, you will find it helpful to read the English policy. If you are supporting pupils with SEN, then you need to read the SEN and the inclusion polices as these will help you to understand the SEN framework.

There will also be a school prospectus, which is a useful first document to read as it provides a lot of basic information about the school. When you first start as a TA, a map of the school, a staffing list and timetable will be invaluable. An annual calendar of events will also help you to understand the cycle of school events. Most schools have a staff handbook, which you will be given as part of your induction and will give you this practical information.

There will also be ongoing procedural changes. It is unlikely that you will attend all staff meetings (which are normally held outside the TA contracted hours), so in order to be aware of week-by-week changes, you need to refer to a member of staff, probably the special needs coordinator, who should make you aware of changes, particularly if they affect you. Watch the noticeboards in the staffroom as these normally show weekly events and updates. Again, *communication* is the key factor. No one likes to feel that they have been left out of a group or that they have missed out on important messages, yet it happens as part of daily routines in the busy daily routines of school life. Try not to take it personally if it happens to you!

'Sorry, did no-one tell you the trip's been postponed until next week?'

By working as part of the learning support, pastoral or curriculum 'team'

Within the school these teams are as described above. The head teacher has overall responsibility for you and may take an active interest, but usually the role of supervision is delegated to the special needs coordinator, the head of subject, and the pastoral head of year or class teacher. The class teacher, or teachers in secondary schools, will be the main person(s) you see most of day-to-day so they will be the ones who direct and supervise a lot of your work. If you are supporting pupils with SEN, you are likely to have regular meetings with the SENCO, who will give you guidance on how best to work with pupils. He or she will also help to train you in delivering specific learning programmes or IT support applications.

There are other professionals whose workbase is outside the school but who come into the school regularly to give advice about pupils with special needs and are therefore part of a wider support network. These include educational psychologists, physiotherapists, occupational therapists, speech and language therapists and advisory teachers. These people will be pleased to discuss with you any relevant issues related to your work (see Appendix B.)

In an ideal situation, you will feel valued and supported if colleagues in the school see you as part of a team. Giving you the opportunity to be involved in planning and decision-making will encourage your own ideas and creativity and you will feel more positive about your role in the school. This depends partly on the attitudes of other members of staff. Occasionally some individuals may find partnership working too threatening and are thus unable to treat you as having a different but equal contribution to make. More usually, however, it is because staff are too busy to step back from their daily work and plan ahead with you. Too often, assistants are placed in a 'reactive' role – responding to what-ever comes up at the time without any planning, rather than a 'proactive' role – taking time to plan intervention in advance. This is changing, as the research indicates that the proactive use of assistants can lead to improved learning and progress.

In order to make the best use of your time, a teamwork approach is vital. Very few teachers would disagree with this. If you feel you are a 'reactive' TA, then discuss with the class teacher and/or special needs coordinator any ideas you might have about improving your use of time and your need to feel part of a team.

Working with parents or carers

The parents or home carers of the pupils needing support also play a part in this teamwork approach. It is important that they are made aware of the programmes and plans which are being made for their children so that they can be encouraged to support the work of the school at home in what-ever way is appropriate. The most important adults in a child's life are the parents and their influence on the child is enormous. It is important that they understand the implications of any difficulties and are helped to be positive in their attitudes and expectations. Your job may bring you into frequent contact with the child's parents or carers, particularly if the child has physical disabilities. In some cases an important part of your role may be to develop a positive relationship with the parents and to foster links between home and school, working in partnership with the class teacher. At times, it may be necessary to provide a 'listening ear' in order to support the parents and to understand what is going on in the child's home life. It is necessary to keep a safe distance emotionally when this happens and to be aware of getting embroiled in complex family dynamics. As discussed earlier in the book, it is also necessary to keep confidences which may be shared. The class teacher should be aware of relevant issues and should be able to intervene should things become too difficult emotionally. Sometimes it is very hard for parents to accept that their child has a special need or is not making the same progress as others. You may have a part to play in help-ing them to come to terms with this and to be realistic. You will need to consider the best way to discuss this with parents in conjunction with other staff members so that everyone is giving the same message. Occasionally parents receive mixed messages from different staff members at school. Valuing what a child is good at and pointing out progress in any area may be part of your role in such a situation.

Contributing to reviews

Every pupil who has a statement of special educational needs or an education, health and care plan (EHC plan) must have a review of their needs, at least annually. This includes a meeting when all concerned with the pupil, both inside the school and outside, can come together, discuss recent reports, inform each other about progress and make plans for meeting the pupil's needs in the future. Pupils without statements or EHC plans often have internal review meetings.

If you have had close contact with the pupil, you may be asked to give a short verbal or written report at the meeting and if you have kept records they will prove useful in giving your report. Do remember that there will always be people within the school who will help you to do this and there will be opportunities for you to discuss your contribution before the meeting.

Occasionally there will be case conferences about children with whom you are involved. Such meetings normally follow a pupil's exclusion from school or some safeguarding concern voiced by the school, health or social services. Again, you may be asked to give your perspective about the pupil's needs. On rare occasions you could be asked to give your views on a child's needs and progress for court hearings. Your teacher colleagues will support you in doing this. It is important that you give your views in line with the school views about the child's needs following preparation and discussion of the issues with teachers.

Attending relevant in-service training or staff meetings

When opportunities arise to further your knowledge about any aspect of teaching and learning or to be involved in meetings about whole-school initiatives, then do try to attend. Ideally, this time should come from within your school hours – in reality many TAs choose to work additional hours so that their pupils do not miss out.

This need for TA training is increasingly recognised and provided for in many areas, although there are still too few opportunities for TAs to get the training they would like.

By using particular personal strengths

The whole class and maybe the school can benefit if you are prepared to share any particular talent you might have. It could be that you are a good singer or can play an instrument well. Perhaps you have an artistic or dramatic talent or maybe your culinary or D.I.Y. skills are renowned. Many assistants help out with school productions and Christmas events and enjoy supporting pupils in these extra-curricular activities.

Don't hide your light under a bushel – be willing to contribute. And don't underestimate the parenting skills you may have – the vast majority of TAs are parents themselves so can often provide insights into what might be appropriate to solve common childhood problems.

"Don't hide your light under a bushel"

Safeguarding

Everyone who comes into contact with children and their families has a role to play in safeguarding children and young people. As a TA, you are particularly important because of your regular contact with pupils, so you might be one of the first to notice any concerning behaviour. Schools and colleges and their staff form part of the wider safeguarding system for children which includes doctors and health visitors, police and social workers.

What do we mean by safeguarding children?

The Department for Education issued statutory guidance on safeguarding in 2015 called 'Keeping children safe in education'.

In this document, safeguarding and promoting the welfare of children is defined as:

- protecting children from maltreatment;
- preventing impairment of children's health or development;
- ensuring that children grow up in circumstances consistent with the provision of safe and effective care;
- taking action to enable all children to have the best outcomes. (NB Children includes everyone under the age of 18.)

It states that:

> *Where a child is suffering significant harm, or is likely to do so, action should be taken to protect that child. Action should also be taken to promote the welfare of a child in need of additional support, even if they are not suffering harm or are at immediate risk.*

As a TA, you should know the systems within your school or college which support safeguarding, and these should be explained to you as part of your induction, where you will be trained in procedures.

If, during the course of your work with a child, some disclosure of physical, emotional or sexual abuse is made to you or you suspect neglect, then you have a duty, under Child Protection Law, to inform the head teacher, who will take any action necessary. The 1989 Children Act states that the child's welfare is paramount and safeguarding it and promoting it is a priority. As a result, there will be a range of checks on your background to make sure that you are not a risk to the pupils. When you apply for the job, the school has a duty to check your details against police lists and the Disclosure and Barring Service (DBS, previously the Criminal Records Bureau) to make sure that you are a fit person to work with children and young people and do not have any criminal convictions. This is a national process which all people who want to work with children must comply with.

Schools have clear routines to be followed in the case of injury or abuse and it is your responsibility to ensure that you know what these procedures are. If you are not sure, the class teacher you normally work with can direct you to the information. This sort of information should be provided as part of your induction. The following are guidelines which are often used in safeguarding courses.

- If a pupil tells you something or you see something which rings an alarm bell, give him or her reassurance, e.g. 'I can see that must have been difficult/scary for you', but do not probe any further at this stage.
- If the pupil says it is a secret then do not promise to keep it. Write the details down as soon after as you can.
- Tell the named teacher, SENCO or head teacher what you have heard or seen. Write the details down as soon after as you can.
- Do not take any action yourself.

In every school there is a named senior teacher for safeguarding (The Designated Safeguarding Lead: DSL). This teacher will be responsible for taking any action required following a disclosure by the pupil, including involving external agencies if there are clear indications of abuse. This teacher will have annual training and ALL staff, including TAs, will have refresher training every three years.

What does this mean for me?

69

What should I be alert to?

Physical abuse

You need to report if you see any signs of physical harm, over and above that of normal cuts and bruises which all children experience from time to time. If you observe any persistent hitting or rough handling by adults you will need to report it. Be aware of unusual patterns of behaviour such as sleepiness, hyperactivity or inability to concentrate as this may be a sign of drug and/or alcohol use.

Emotional abuse

You need to report any awareness of emotional maltreatment of the child. This may include bullying, cyberbullying or causing children to feel frightened or in danger. The child may become unusually withdrawn and quiet or might start acting up.

Sexual abuse

You need to report any indication that the child is being sexually exploited or forced to participate in sexual activities. This may involve internet activity. Often, victims of such abuse become withdrawn or exhibit disturbing behaviour.

Neglect

You need to report any indication that the child's basic needs are not being met, e.g. lack of food, inadequate clothing or lack of access to the home after school, or abandonment. Some children become carers for disabled parents or siblings and this can sometimes, though not always, lead to the child having responsibilities they cannot manage.

The Prevent duty

The Department for Education published advice to schools in 2015 called the Prevent duty. This means that school staff are able to identify children and young people who may be vulnerable to radicalisation. It was brought in to address concerns that a small minority of young people are being taught extremist views which are not aligned with traditional British values.

> (ref: See *The Prevent Duty. Departmental advice for schools and childcare providers.* DfE 2015c.)

Activity

Take a look at each of these aspects and note what you might need to do to be more effective.

- Supporting the school values and ethos;
- Knowing the school policies and procedures;

- By working as part of the learning support, pastoral or curriculum team;
- Working with parents or carers;
- Contributing to reviews;
- Attending in-service training or staff meetings;
- By using particular personal strengths.

Safeguarding.

- Do you understand what is included in safeguarding children?
- What is your role?
- What do you need to be alert to?

Promoting effective learning

Chapter summary

- Ways in which children learn
    - Practical experience
    - Using all senses
    - Relating new experiences to previous learning
    - Developing understanding through talking
    - Moving across subject boundaries
    - Planning and reflection
    - Repetition, practice and reinforcement
    - High expectations and clear learning goals
- Learning styles
    - Auditory
    - Visual
    - Kinaesthetic
- What stops pupils from learning?
- Learning difficulties
- Understanding learning
    - Bloom's taxonomy
    - Mindset
- Activity

Over recent years there has been an increasing focus on raising standards in schools and, as a result, teaching assistants (TAs) need to be more aware and informed about their role in promoting the learning and progress of pupils. This doesn't mean moving away from a more nurturing role, but to be aware that the role now requires more knowledge and understanding of how children and young people learn and how best to give support to the learning process.

Learning is essential to our survival! If you think of a new-born baby, it has needs for food, warmth and sleep. Babies are pretty good at letting us know when they need something – determining what *exactly* they need can sometimes be difficult! However, the baby quickly learns how to get attention in order to get their needs met. As the baby grows, he or she will start exploring the environment and through daily experiences will learn about how to survive and enjoy the surrounding world. Children are naturally curious and will quickly learn what to do in order to have good experiences rather than bad. Touching a hot pan will result in a hasty recoil and a learning experience which says beware of hot pans. Finding that it is fun to knock a tower of bricks down encourages the child to repeat the experience and rebuild the tower.

Ways in which children learn

The following principles, put together by the Hampshire Inspection and Advisory Support Service (1992) are fundamental statements about learning and are true for all children.

- Children learn primarily through practical first-hand experiences.
- Children learn through all their senses (with the rare exception of children who have severe sensory impairment).
- Children make sense of new experiences by relating them to previous learning.
- Children develop their understanding through talking.
- Children may move across subject boundaries as they learn.
- Children learn best when they can make sense of what they do through involvement in planning and reflection.
- Children learn through purposeful repetition, practice and reinforcement.
- Children learn best when there is care, tolerance, security, praise and high expectations, associated with clear learning goals.
- Children have preferred learning styles and learn at different rates.

Children learn primarily through practical first-hand experiences

Young children find many opportunities to play, and through play they begin to recognise objects and how they work. Manipulating sand, playing with water, sorting stones or shells and playing with commercially produced toys enables the child to develop basic concepts. Usually this starts with ideas of object permanence at around eight months when young children will look for an object that is covered up, getting the idea of objects being there even though they are not seen. Words such as 'all gone' start to have meaning. Basic ideas of colour and shape are learned and concepts such as up/down, in/out, big/little are among the first to develop in children. If adults around them provide the language to support and guide play and to describe what the child is doing then this helps children to learn at a faster rate. This use of language is very important in enabling the child to learn, because effective understanding and use of language are crucial to the later development of both literacy and numeracy. There are important early concepts which support children's understanding of number, for example, same and different, more and less, bigger and smaller, are all basic concepts which help our understanding of number.

The skill of classification, i.e. sorting into groups those items with similar characteristics, is an important skill in the development of both literacy and numeracy.

So we can see how practical first-hand experiences enable learning but this is not just at an early stage. It is always helpful to use equipment when introducing new ideas to older children. Many of them lose the need for these props to learning as they become more able to use written words and numbers, but for children who find it difficult then the use of practical toys, apparatus and equipment will aid understanding.

Children learn through all their senses

We have five senses: sight, hearing, touch, smell and taste. We have already seen how young children use touch, sight and hearing to develop new ideas. Young children are also quite good at exploring their environment through taste and smell, particularly in relation to their feeding behaviour! The senses of sight, hearing and touch are important for early language development. As the child becomes more proficient, the senses of sight and hearing are the two main senses used in literacy and numeracy. If the child shows some difficulties in learning how to read, write or learn numbers, then a 'multi-sensory' approach is often recommended, which means using more than one channel to support learning. (Learning styles are discussed later in this chapter.)

Children make sense of new experiences by relating them to previous learning

The renowned child psychologist, Jean Piaget, developed a theory of children's learning which includes the notions of *assimilation* and *accommodation*. Assimilation is when a child takes in some information from the environment, stores it and uses it as the need arises. Through play the child assimilates or 'gathers in' a great deal of information.

Accommodation is when a 'correction' has to be applied to the original concept or idea as a result of a new experience, and a modification or a change made to a previous view. So children, as they learn new things, build on previous learning experiences. To give an example, if a child wanted a biscuit and the parent had decided to move the place where the biscuits were kept, then the child, not knowing this, would search in the cupboard where, from previous experience, they had learned the biscuits would be. Not finding them, they might give up or, depending on how hungry they were, search other cupboards on the principle that the biscuits would be kept in a similar place. On finding the biscuits they would learn the new location and probably remember it the next time they wanted a biscuit!

Children who are learning to read are constantly revising their word knowledge. A child who knows the word 'bend' might then apply their learning and be able to recognise 'mend'. A child who knows the word 'cough' might logically pronounce the word 'bough' as 'boff' but would then have to learn that there are a number of ways to pronounce the group of letters 'ough' (i.e. cough, bough, enough, ought).

In learning what numbers are, there is a sequence of prerequisite skills and ideas which need to be in place before the child can do this effectively, e.g. in knowing what 'two' means, a child must know it is more than one, less than three, and that the word 'two' can be used with any objects where there are two of that object together, i.e. two elephants, two sweets; this idea is called 1 to 1 correspondence.

In all our learning, we build on what we already know. Therefore, in any new learning it is important to gain an understanding of what the pupil already knows so that *the next step* can be taught. This makes it important that the task presented to a pupil is at the right level and matched to the ability level of the child so that a successful learning experience takes place.

Children develop their understanding through talking

If you have ever watched a young child at play you will notice that he or she uses quite a lot of noise and occasionally words alongside their action – it seems to be a natural thing to do. Their play seems first to affect language as children 'commentate' on their actions and then as they grow older language starts to affect play. Much has been written over the years both by philosophers and psychologists about the important relationship between thought and language.

Questions have been asked about how thought affects language and how language guides thoughts and perceptions. It is said, for instance, that the Inuit population have several different words for 'snow', each of which describes a different sort of snow. Does knowing those words then affect the way they observe and experience snow? If we had the words too, would our perception of snow be enhanced? There is undoubtedly a link between understanding language and being able to structure and make sense of our environment, and there is evidence that good language structures enable faster and more effective processing of information.

An experiment is described in which young children were presented with a wooden board with holes into which cylinders of different sizes are designed to fit. The experimenters found that children who understood concepts and knew the words for tall/short, fat/thin, wide/narrow were quicker at doing the task than the children who did not seem to understand the words which describe size. The children with an understanding of several size concepts: fat/thin, tall/short, wide/narrow were quicker than children who understood only big/little as descriptions of size.

These examples demonstrate how language provides a structure for effective thinking. The child who develops language skills without difficulty is likely to go on to learn to read without difficulty and to understand mathematical ideas without difficulty. It is often the children who find it hard to grasp the structure and meaning of language who struggle later with the development of literacy and numeracy skills.

You will note in your work that, for pupils who do seem to find work difficult, a number of them will have been seen by a speech and language therapist at an earlier stage or parents will report that they appeared slow to develop language skills. For some reason, possibly linked to genetic factors, boys are more affected than girls. Many more boys than girls have slow language development in the early years and there are more boys than girls in our schools who require additional support in the area of literacy or dyslexia. This early difference narrows to a large extent as children get older, but there are clear gender differences in the early years.

This influence of language on thought processes has considerable implications for your work, as it demonstrates the importance of understanding basic language skills and concepts before the child can learn to read or manipulate numbers. For young children you can check which concepts and ideas they already know and help identify the gaps in their knowledge.

For older children, again you will need to check understanding and not make assumptions that the language concepts necessary for learning a new task are in place.

Children may move across subject boundaries as they learn

Just because literacy and numeracy are taught regularly in schools does not mean that these skills are not being taught through other subjects or at other times in the school day. Indeed, you can make links and help pupils see that, for example, the key words in a history topic are similar to other words used in other lessons, that sentence constructions, layout of work, etc., are common across many subjects. Similarly, ideas of shape, weight and size can be recognised in subjects other than maths and the general skill of classification, useful for all learning, occurs right across the curriculum. This is called generalisation and demonstrates the ability to learn a skill or concept in one subject and apply it effectively in another.

Children learn best when they can make sense of what they do through involvement in planning and reflection

Everyone likes to be involved in the planning of activities which will affect them. If you were planning an extension to your house you would want to have your views taken into account when the planning was being done because you know what will and what won't work and 'fit' with your style of living. It is the same with learning. Children are much more likely to get the best 'fit' with their learning if you can involve them in planning the work. If they feel they have some control over what they do then they are far more likely to become engaged with the task. Even a simple choice like 'which task shall we do first?' is helpful because the pupil does not feel passive in the process of learning.

This is especially important for pupils experiencing learning difficulties as it is all too easy for the pupil to 'take a back seat' and let the assistant do the work. Most lessons include a time for reflection, *the plenary session*, at the end. The process of reflection on work done, i.e. 'How well did I do it?', 'How might I have done it better?' is also crucial in enabling the pupil to learn. Your role in this is to provide feedback, and doing this can be quite a skilled job if the pupil's self-esteem is to be maintained (see Chapter 4 for a feedback form example). Pupils who struggle with learning may be uncertain about their ability to do well, so require plenty of encouragement and reassurance. It is always important in giving feedback to find something positive to say before asking the pupil to self-correct their work. If they cannot see what is wrong you will need to point it out using phrases such as 'Jack, you're doing well with this, try putting another "p" in here, that will make it right'.

Looking at examples of how others have presented work can also be helpful, although it can be de-motivating if the pupil sees work of a standard they think they could never attain!

Children learn through purposeful repetition, practice and reinforcement

If you play a musical instrument, you will recall that there was a time when you could not do it. An intensive period of learning new skills was necessary in order to get to the point where you were ready to play independently. As you were learning, there was a need for lots of practice, repetition and reinforcement, the 'making stronger' of the correct actions and thinking which actions combine together to make you into a successful musician. There is also a time element which is significant. If your lessons were six months apart then you would forget a good deal between lessons and would have to start from scratch again. Most people learning an instrument have lessons at least once a week so that skills can be practised, learned and reinforced. This relates to the way our memories work.

It is acknowledged that there are two types of memory: short-term and long-term, and that, for true learning to take place, information must pass from our short-term memory into our long-term memory, and if there is too great a time lapse then this does not happen and learning does not take place.

So it is with the learning of reading, writing, spelling and number skills. Children need to practise these skills often if they are to learn effectively. For pupils who learn at a slower pace than others this is even more important, and much repetition is required for information to 'stick'.

Take the skill of learning to read, which requires a combination of subskills. The majority of children learn to read using a pattern of practice and reinforcement which seems to work. However, there are some children subjected to the same 'treatment' who fail to make progress. What is happening? Why don't they learn?

A project in Essex called the 'Early Reading Research' project has attempted to change patterns of instruction for children and has shown that certain ways of using repetition, practice and reinforcement can be particularly effective with all children, including children who previously might have had difficulties in learning to read. This particular project has shown that significant improvements in children's reading can be made by using a number of principles which do work.

- *Distributed practice* – the researchers found that 'little and often' works much better than longer periods of work at more widely spaced intervals. For children learning to read, short periods of daily practice or even twice daily practice is better than longer periods of work once or twice a week. This is because information in the child's short-term memory is reinforced before it is 'lost' and is therefore more likely to pass into the long-term memory.

- *Interleaved practice* – the researchers also found that learning new words alongside words already learned was more effective than just learning new words alone. This technique seems to help children to remember learned material so the child would, for example, learn ten words, then another three, then practise all thirteen, learn another three, practise all sixteen, etc.

Children learn best when there is care, tolerance, security, praise and high expectation associated with clear learning goals

Picture a scene in which a young child is starting to walk. There may be parents or relatives around smiling, clapping, cheering and urging the child on. When the child manages to take the first few hesitant steps, there are celebrations and approval and the child gets big smiles from the 'audience'. 'Good boy, now walk to Daddy'. If the child were to fall after a step or two, no-one would dream of saying 'No, that's wrong', or 'Get up you lazy boy and do as I say!' So, most adults start off brilliantly as carers and encouragers of children, setting clear expectations of the next step, in this case quite literally! What we need to remember is that children of all ages are learning new skills all the time and they need encouragement at every stage.

Unfortunately, this positive approach seems to fall away for some children as they grow. This sometimes happens as the child becomes more difficult to control or when the adult gets frustrated because the child won't do as he or she is asked. This can happen with learning to read and write, particularly if the adult working with the child expects too much. It can be easy to blame the child sometimes rather than the task or the teacher.

When negative messages are given to a child at an early stage then an unhealthy cycle of 'can't do, won't do' seems to emerge. The child finds it hard to read, the adults give a negative message to the child, the child then thinks negatively of themselves in relation to reading and starts to dislike the experience of reading, viewing themselves as unsuccessful in the task.

The first years at school are important for all children. For those who may be 'at risk' of finding learning difficult, e.g. those who have had some language or social difficulties at a preschool stage, they are especially important. Particular attention needs to be paid to ensuring that these children do not start to see themselves as failures.

Patience, tolerance and positive regard for children are key qualities of teachers and assistants, especially at this important stage of development. (In Chapter 3 'Supporting the Pupil', the importance of care, tolerance and praise are discussed in greater detail.) You will need to remember that children constantly need approval and thrive on encouragement and praise. This can be demonstrated in a number of ways and can be non-verbal, such as a smile, a nod of the head or a pat on the back, or it can be verbal, using positive comments about the learning behaviour which you observe. Visual feedback is also valuable, particularly for children with poor memories. Tokens of approval such as stars on a chart, 'smiley face' stickers or positive notes home or to the teacher or head teacher can be really effective in motivating the child to learn.

Learning styles

If you have children of your own, you will be aware that, even with children from similar genetic backgrounds, there are quite marked differences in the ways children develop and learn. Each child has their own personality and predisposition to learning, each their own particular strengths and weaknesses. There is, from time to time, a debate about the relative influences on our development of 'nature', i.e. what we are born with and 'nurture' – the effects of our families and environment. Most writers accept that it seems to be a combination of both which guides the way we grow, think and learn.

Some of these individual characteristics, especially physical characteristics, appear fixed, e.g. shape of ear, hair colour, but some can be influenced by family experience, e.g. a child from a non-nurturing family background may become emotionally troubled and this will have an effect on how they learn as children. Those who are unsettled in their home lives seem to also find it difficult to 'settle' to learning.

As part of these individual differences, it is recognised that there are different 'learning styles', and by this we mean that there are several channels of communication into a child's mind, and we need to determine which one is best for them.

The idea cross references with multi-sensory learning and, in order to identify a child's preferred 'learning style', it is necessary to find out, by observation, trial and error what works best for each child.

Three main learning styles have been identified: auditory, visual and kinaesthetic. Most children can use all three but some have one which they use more than others.

Auditory learners

As the name suggests, these are pupils who learn best through hearing, so they absorb information best by listening to others or by hearing internally as they read. These pupils are usually good at language and interested in words and meanings. They will be good at conversation and expressing themselves by talking. In lessons, they will be able to remember teacher directions and retain any facts presented as the teacher talks. This group of pupils are usually good at academic subjects and do well in school.

Visual learners

These pupils learn best if there is a visual clue or stimulus to support learning activities. So they find it easier to look at a picture or diagram in a book before attempting to read. They learn more easily if there are charts, diagrams, pictures or videos to support new information. They find it helpful to see or visualise the end product, e.g. in food technology or craft activities. They are often creative pupils who can see links where others cannot.

Many visual learners benefit from learning the technique of 'mind-mapping' – when they can link ideas on paper using coloured lines and bubbles to help them to visualise links and learning sequences. As a TA, learning how to do mind-mapping will help you to support these pupils.

Kinaesthetic learners

These pupils learn best through active, practical experiences where they can feel and manipulate equipment. So it helps if younger children can use interlocking cubes to help with maths or plastic letters to feel the shapes of words or trace them in sand. Older students enjoy practical subjects like design and technology or art and some go on to do practical jobs when they leave school. Sometimes these pupils are frustrated by a high level of auditory input so, as a TA, you need to be creative in finding ways of including practical activities or drawing to support learning.

What stops pupils from learning?

As we have seen, negative messages to pupils or failure in a task can hinder their learning by lowering confidence. There are usually several factors which interact to prevent effective learning. These might include:

- negative feedback;
- frequent absence from school;
- limited preschool experience;
- poor language development;

- poor teaching methods;
- expectations too high;
- expectations too low;
- distracting learning environment;
- poor timing of teaching input;
- lack of recognition of pupil's preferred learning style;
- insufficient consideration of how much teaching repetition and practice is needed;
- not enough thought about when is the best time of day for certain types of learning to take place;
- not enough consideration of where the pupil is likely to learn best, e.g. in small groups or whole-class work;
- how much the pupil is encouraged or discouraged by others;
- how much encouragement the pupil needs from the teacher and the assistant.

Teachers and assistants must always be ready to change or modify the task so that the pupil *can* learn. This is often done 'on the hoof' but can be discussed when reviewing the individual learning programme, and remember:

- realistic objectives should be set – be clear about the capabilities of the pupil and don't expect too much, or too little!
- learning activities should be matched to the ability of the pupil so success is assured;
- learning should be planned in small steps with frequent repetition – go over what has been taught often so that the pupil does not forget;
- a wide variety of materials and opportunities to learn through first-hand experiences is necessary – learning through doing.

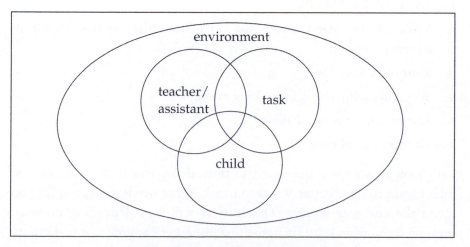

Interacting factors in the learning situation

We see then that there are many components to effective learning and interacting factors which need to be considered. The above diagram illustrates this. The factors are:

- the nature of the pupil – attitude, abilities, prior learning, etc.;
- the nature of the task presented;
- the way the task is taught;
- the learning environment – arrangement of class, peer group, etc.

Learning difficulties

We hear a lot about children's 'learning difficulties'. The Code of Practice (2015) framework means that some children are categorised as having mild, moderate, specific or severe learning difficulties (see Chapter 9).

It is important to view learning difficulties as a relative term.

Remember:

'If the tasks and activities in which the learning is engaged are not matched to the learner's capabilities, or are not understood by the learner, then learning difficulties are likely to occur.'

(Ainscow and Tweddle, 1988)

The importance of matching the task to the child is made very clear in the 1981 Education Act. This stresses that 'special educational needs' is a relative term which arises from the interaction between a child and his or her environment. By planning realistic and achievable learning tasks, learning difficulties can be avoided. As a TA you are there to work with the teacher to remove the 'barriers' to learning.

Imagine that you are given a task to do. The task is to follow a complicated recipe to produce a lemon soufflé within a set time limit. What might stop you from doing this well?

- You haven't got the right ingredients.
- You can't understand the metric weight system.
- You don't like lemons.
- You can't understand some of the instructions (they are translated from a French version).
- Your oven has a fault.
- You don't whip the eggs for long enough.
- The container is too shallow.
- You run out of time.

Let's look at what was stopping you from doing this right and how you might learn to do it better. We need to ask 'What needs to happen for you to do the task successfully?' The answers will vary depending on what prevented you from learning in the first place. Let's assume that you can do this task given the right conditions and support.

Consider the barriers to successful learning and how to remove them:

Barriers to learning	Solution
Wrong ingredients	Plan ahead, make sure you have them
Metric weights	Ask for a weight conversion table
Don't like lemons	Make a chocolate soufflé
Can't understand instructions	Ask for help
Faulty oven	Arrange to get it fixed
Eggs not whipped enough	Whip eggs for longer
Wrong container	Use a deeper container
Out of time	Learn to work faster or ask for more time

As you will note, the task would have been much easier if some preparations had been made so that the conditions were right for you to be successful. What is also clear in this kind of learning is that a demonstration of how to do this, step by step, would have been particularly helpful.

Consider what would have happened had your soufflé flopped. Most likely you would not view yourself as a successful maker of soufflés and you would be unwilling to have another go. Your motivation would diminish. If you could have done it but ran out of time you would feel frustrated by the time limit.

Consider too how you would feel if you were making the soufflé in the same room with others who had more success than you. You may feel annoyed or frustrated that others could do this while you could not.

This teaches us that, for learning to be effective:

- The correct tools for the job need to be prepared.
- Visual prompts can be very useful.
- The preferred learning style should be used.
- Sticking points should be anticipated.
- The rate or pace of learning should be taken into account – allow enough time for success.
- Repetition and practice are needed – work out how much and when.
- Encouragement is essential – we all need it.
- The effects of the environment and peer group need to be considered.
- Tasks should be demonstrated (have a go yourself!).

Show the child how to do it by having a go yourself

Understanding learning

There are many studies about how children learn but two approaches have been particularly influential in the last ten years.

1 Bloom's Taxonomy

The work of Benjamin Bloom, an educational psychologist working in the 1950s, has been used by many teachers to understand how people think

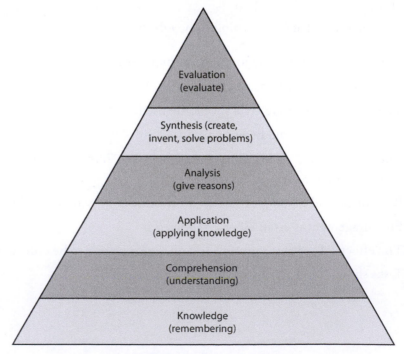

Bloom's Taxonomy

and learn. So it will be helpful if you, as a TA, know something about this as it can help your understanding of the learning process and can give practical support to the way you work with pupils, particularly in the way you use questioning.

A taxonomy is a classification or arrangement of data, or processes in this case.
We can see how this works in practice by using an example of each level of in the triangle, ranging from the simplest level of learning: knowledge, at the base, to the most complex level: evaluation at the apex.

Knowledge: Recalling facts and information, e.g. how many different kinds of tree can you name?

Comprehension: Showing understanding by explaining, e.g. where do different kinds of trees grow? How do they grow?

Application: Applying previous knowledge and understanding in new learning, e.g. how are trees used in everyday life?

Analysis: Breaking down information to component parts and analysing the relationship between each, e.g. what are the similarities between evergreen and deciduous trees? What are the differences?

Synthesis: Applying previous learning in a new way to create original ideas, e.g. how might rainforests be preserved in the future?

Evaluation: Judging information using personal reflection to justify an approach, e.g. when and why might it be justifiable to challenge the management of tree clearance by some governments?

2 Mindset

Another American psychologist, Carole Dweck, has published a book called *Mindset: The New Psychology of Success*. In it, she describes an experiment using a group of primary age children who teachers described as helpless … ones who gave up easily when they thought maths problems were too hard. Through a series of exercises, the experimenters trained half of the group to attribute their failures to insufficient effort, and encouraged them to keep going. Given the right encouragement, these children learned to persist with the maths problems, and succeed. No special support was given to the other half of the group, who continued to give up easily and fail the tasks. This shows that if children think that they cannot do a task because it is too hard, or they are likely to fail, they will soon give up. However, if they can be trained to believe that it is not that they cannot do it, but they have not tried hard enough, the likelihood of success is improved. So, 'mindset' (a positive attitude to learning) has been shown to be important in the learning process.

Activity

- Think of an activity you cannot do yet, or are not very good at. This could be following a knitting pattern, driving a car, growing a vegetable garden, learning a musical instrument.
- Ask yourself, 'What needs to happen for me to learn this activity successfully?'
- Write a list of the barriers to learning.
- Next to each 'barrier', think of a solution which would overcome the barrier.
- Think of a pupil you work with and list the barriers he or she faces in any learning task.
- Next to each barrier, think of a solution which would overcome the barrier.

In doing this task, you may be able to identify your own learning style and that of the pupil.

CHAPTER 8

Special educational needs

Chapter summary

- The special educational needs framework
  - What is meant by 'special educational needs'?
  - What is the 'Code of Practice'?
  - Code of Practice 2015
  - Code of Practice Principles
- School procedures
  - What should schools do to support pupils with special educational needs?
  - Changes in school procedures
  - What is 'School Support' as defined in the Code of Practice?
  - What is an Individual Learning Programme/Individual Education Plan? (ILP/IEP)
  - What is an 'Education, Health and Care Plan'?
  - How are special educational needs identified?
  - The importance of early identification
  - Assessment of pupils (see also Chapter 5)
  - Does the pupil need additional support?
- What can affect SEN?
  - External factors
  - Pupils with English as an additional language
  - The quality of teaching
- Monitoring and reviewing progress
  - Who should be informed?
  - Who is responsible for pupils with SEN?
  - When should progress be reviewed?
  - Transition arrangements
- Activity

The special educational needs framework

In your work as a teaching assistant (TA) it will be helpful for you to understand some of the background and the framework which underpins the way pupils identified as having special needs are supported in our schools.

What is meant by 'special educational needs'?

The 1981 Education Act states that: '*A child has special educational needs if he or she has a learning difficulty which may be a result of a physical or sensory disability, an emotional or behavioural problem or developmental delay*' (1981 Education Act, Section 1).

This significant act helped to change ideas about children with difficulties. Before the 1981 Act, children had been categorised and labelled according to their 'handicap'. People had referred to children with such labels as 'physically handicapped', 'mentally handicapped', 'educationally sub-normal' or 'maladjusted'.

The 1981 Act:

- changed the focus away from labelling the child;
- placed the focus on the extent to which a learning difficulty stops a child from learning with other children of the same age;
- placed the focus on the child's special educational needs in terms of the special educational provision required to help them learn;
- stressed that 'special educational needs' is a relative term which arises from the interaction between a child and his or her environment.

The idea of a child's needs being related to the school's ability to meet the needs was a new perspective which helped teachers understand that difficulties in learning do not always start from within the child. All children can learn, although sometimes the child does not learn because the school does not provide the learning tasks or levels of support which are necessary for learning to take place and sometimes needs are, in fact, created because the school is not able to be flexible. Thus the *interaction* between the child and his or her learning environment is now considered crucial in any discussion about special educational needs.

Children who have special educational needs (SEN) are described under four broad areas:

- communication and interaction
- cognition and learning
- social, emotional and mental health
- sensory and/or physical

(See Chapters 9 and 10 for more details on how to support these needs.)

The purpose of identifying these areas of need is to work out what action the school needs to take, not to fit a pupil into a category. In practice, individual children or young people often have needs that cut across all these areas and their needs may change over time. For instance speech, language and communication needs can also be a feature of a number of other areas of SEN, and children and young people with an autistic spectrum disorder (ASD) may have needs across all areas, including particular sensory requirements. A detailed multi-agency assessment of need should ensure that the full range of needs is identified, including health and social care needs, not simply the primary need. Additional help, often supported by a TA, should address all needs using effective interventions, using specialist equipment or software if appropriate.

The Code of Practice on the identification and assessment of special educational needs is statutory guidance, i.e. schools must follow it, and was first published by the DfE, or DfES as it then was (Department for Education and Science) in 1994 to give practical guidance to local authorities (LAs) and to the governing bodies of all maintained schools on their responsibilities towards children with special educational needs. Since then there have been two revisions and updates.

What is the 'Code of Practice'?

Code of Practice 2015

In 2014 the Code was revised, and was issued jointly in 2015 by the Department for Education and the Department of Health as the 'Special Educational Needs and Disability Code of Practice 0–25 years'. There are several changes from the previous 2001 Code as follows:

- The Code of Practice 2015 covers the 0–25 age range.

- There is a clearer focus on the views of children and young people and their role in decision-making.

- It includes guidance on the joint planning and commissioning of services to ensure close co-operation between education, health services and social care.

- For children and young people with more complex needs, a coordinated assessment process and the new *0–25 Education, Health and Care Plan* (EHC Plan) replaces statements and Learning Difficulty Assessments.

- There is new guidance on the support pupils and students should receive in education and training settings.

- There is a greater focus on support that enables those with SEN to succeed in their education and make a successful transition to adulthood.

The code makes it very clear that the majority of children and young people with SEN will attend mainstream nurseries, schools and colleges and will *not* need an Education, Health and Care plan, which is only for pupils with severe or complex long-term needs. It states that schools must use their 'best endeavours' to ensure that they make the necessary arrangements and put in the right level of support for any child or young person who has SEN.

Code of Practice Principles

The Code of Practice 2015 describes the following principles and it is important for TAs to understand these principles, as well as teachers and senior managers.

These principles are about:

- The *participation* of children, their parents and young people in decision-making.
- The *early identification* of children and young people's needs and early intervention to support them.
- Greater *choice* and control for young people and parents over support.
- *Collaboration* between education, health and social care services to provide support.
- *High-quality provision* to meet the needs of children and young people with SEN.
- A focus on *inclusive practice* and removing barriers to learning.
- Successful *preparation for adulthood*, including independent living and employment.

School procedures

What should schools do to support pupils with special educational needs?

The Code is very clear that all schools and early years settings should have high aspirations and expectations for children and young people with SEN.

This is what the Code says:

'*All children and young people are entitled to an appropriate education, one that is appropriate to their needs, promotes high standards and the fulfilment of potential. This should enable them to:*

- *achieve their best*
- *become confident individuals living fulfilling lives, and*
- *make a successful transition into adulthood, whether into employment, further or higher education or training*

Every school is required to identify and address the SEN of the pupils that they support. Mainstream schools, which includes nursery schools, 16 to 19 academies, alternative provision academies and Pupil Referral Units (PRUs), must:

- *use their best endeavours to make sure that a child with SEN gets the support they need – this means doing everything they can to meet children and young people's SEN*
- *ensure that children and young people with SEN engage in the activities of the school alongside pupils who do not have SEN*
- *designate a teacher to be responsible for coordinating SEN provision – the SEN coordinator, or SENCO*

- *inform parents when they are making special educational provision for a child*

- *prepare an SEN information report and their arrangements for the admission of disabled children, the steps being taken to prevent disabled children from being treated less favourably than others, the facilities provided to enable access to the school for disabled children and their accessibility plan showing how they plan to improve access progressively over time.'*

Changes in school procedures

Until the SEN and Disability Code of Practice 2015, schools were required to set out a 'graduated response' to meeting children's needs and these steps were described as 'school (or early years) action' and 'school (or early years) action plus'. Statements could be requested for those with significant needs beyond those identified as school action plus. The 2015 Code changed this process, replacing 'school (or early years) action' and 'school (or early years) action plus' with the single category of *'school support'* or *'early years support'*. If a child is not making appropriate progress after help under these arrangements, the parents/carers or school can request a 'statutory assessment' which may lead to the issuing of an *Education, Health and Care Plan (EHC plan)*, formerly a statement, but this is *only* for children and young people who have severe and complex long term needs.

The pupil will be described as needing 'school support' or 'early years support' if he or she is not making progress in spite of the class teacher giving more attention and differentiated work (this means work that is matched to his or her ability as discussed in Chapter 5). An important part of the process when identifying a pupil as needing school support is to share concerns with the child's parents/carers to find out if they have extra information about the child and to involve them where possible in actively supporting his/her educational development. The special educational needs coordinator (SENCO) will usually become involved and suggest to the teacher ways in which the pupil can be helped – possibly including some additional support from a TA. An Individual Learning Programme (ILP), or an Individual Education Plan (IEP), will be drawn up to focus on specific targets for the child. There are a range of different names for such plans, e.g. in some secondary schools, these are called student learning profiles (SLPs). When the plan is for supporting behaviour it may be called an individual behaviour plan (IBP) or a pastoral support plan (PSP). Where it is appropriate, the SENCO may contact one or more specialists from outside agencies. These may be professionals from the Local Authority support services, area Health Authority, Social Services and/or independent consultants, e.g. educational psychologists, speech therapists, literacy consultants, learning support advisors and behaviour management consultants. Where more than one specialist is consulted they should work together as a team with the school and the child's parents, to devise and

What is 'School Support' as defined in the Code of Practice?

implement a programme. These outside consultants will often carry out detailed assessments of the child's needs and then advise staff about an appropriate course of action, with targets and a system for monitoring progress. It is rare for them to become directly involved in teaching a child; the class teacher and/or SENCO is usually responsible for the delivery of interventions, often with input from an assistant.

What is an Individual Learning Programme/ Individual Education Plan? (ILP/IEP)

This is a teaching and learning plan for the child, usually drawn up by the SEN coordinator working with the child's teacher, the TA, and possibly with ideas from parents, advisory teachers or educational psychologists. In your school it may be called something different.

According to the Code of Practice the plan should include the following:

- the nature of the child's learning difficulties;
- proposed action:
    - the special educational provision;
    - staff involved, including frequency of support;
    - specific programmes/activities/materials/equipment;
- any help from parents at home;
- the targets to be achieved in a given time;
- any pastoral care or medical requirements;
- the monitoring and assessment arrangements;
- the review arrangements and date.

The recommendation is that the plan should be frequently reviewed to see if it is working well. If not, then the targets and special arrangements should be changed.

The Code guides schools in providing support from their own resources for the vast majority of children with special educational needs and advocates multi-disciplinary assessment *only* for pupils who have severe and complex needs. In spite of a range of specialist support, there may come a point when everyone concerned with the pupil decides that he or she is not making sufficient progress and a statutory assessment of need may be requested. This may or may not lead to an *'Education, Health and Care Plan'*, a legal document which specifies the 'additional' or 'special' resources to be provided for the child or young person. Many assistants work for some or all of their time with pupils who have statements and in the future they will work with pupils who have EHC plans.

It is part of a Local Authority's (LA) duty to consider every application for a statutory assessment, but they may turn down a request if it is not backed up by evidence from the school that appropriate steps have already been taken to help the child at the 'School Support' stage. The school should provide details of the education plans used with the pupil, records of regular reviews, details of attainment in learning (especially literacy and numeracy), views of the parents/carers and of the child, reports from external agencies and medical history where appropriate. If the LA agrees on a statutory, multi-disciplinary assessment, new reports are requested from the educational psychologist and all the other agencies involved with the child, including a school medical officer. All of this information is considered by the LA panel who then decide whether or not to issue an EHC plan. When a plan is written, it usually specifies an amount and the type of help the pupil should receive in school that requires significant additional resources, or it recommends a place in a specialist school or unit. The parents have a right to appeal against any decision made by the LA which they do not agree with, at any stage of the process. If any disagreement cannot be resolved, the case may be referred to the Special Educational Needs Tribunal for a decision to be made.

How are special educational needs identified?

The Code states that all schools should have a clear approach to identifying and responding to SEN. A pupil has SEN where their learning difficulty or disability requires special educational provision, i.e. provision different from or additional to that normally available to pupils of the same age. This is where TAs are often used, to provide that which is 'additional to' what is normally provided working together with the class teacher. Schools should assess each pupil's current skills and levels of attainment on entry, building on information from previous settings and key stages where appropriate. Also, schools should consider whether a pupil may have a disability under the Equality Act 2010 and, if so, what 'reasonable adjustments' may need to be made for them. This can include modifications to the school building as well as the curriculum.

The Code states that, in identifying a child as needing SEN support, the class or subject teacher, working with the SENCO, should carry out a clear

What is an 'Education, Health and Care Plan'?

analysis of the pupil's needs. This should draw on the teacher's assessment and experience of the pupil, their previous progress and attainment, as well as information from the school's pupil progress data on attainment and behaviour. It should also draw on other subject teachers' assessments where relevant, the pupil's development in comparison to other pupils and national data, the views and experience of parents, the pupil's own views (TAs can play a useful part in supporting the pupil in providing this information) and, if relevant, advice from external support services. Schools should take seriously any concerns raised by a parent.

The importance of early identification

The benefits of early identification are widely recognised – identifying need at the earliest point and then making effective provision improves long-term outcomes for the child or young person. For some children, SEN is easily identifiable at an early age. However, for other children and young people, difficulties become evident only as they develop. All those who work with children and young people should be alert to emerging difficulties and respond early. Parents know their children best and it is important that all professionals listen and understand when parents express concerns about their child's development. They should also listen to and address any concerns raised by children and young people themselves. Short-term disruptive or withdrawn behaviours do not necessarily mean that a child or young person has SEN. Where there are concerns, there should be an assessment to determine what is causing the problem, e.g. undiagnosed learning difficulties, difficulties with communication or mental health issues. If it is thought housing, family or other domestic circumstances may be contributing to the difficulties then a multi-agency approach may be appropriate. In all cases, early identification and appropriate support can significantly reduce the use of more costly intervention at a later stage.

Assessment of pupils (see also Chapter 5)

The Code states that class and subject teachers should make regular assessments of progress for all pupils. These should seek to identify pupils making less than expected progress given their age and individual circumstances. The first response to any slower progress should be high-quality teaching targeted at their areas of weakness. Where progress continues to be less than expected the class or subject teacher, working with the SENCO, should assess whether the child has SEN. While informally gathering evidence (including the views of the pupil and their parents) schools should not delay in putting in place extra teaching or other rigorous interventions designed to secure better progress, where required (TAs often help in this respect). The pupil's response to such support can help identify their particular needs.

Any assessments of pupils identified as having SEN should be reviewed regularly and the TA may be a part of this review. Reviews help ensure that support and intervention are matched to need, barriers to learning are identified and overcome, and that everyone has a clear understanding of expected outcomes.

In deciding whether to make special arrangements, the teacher and SENCO will consider all of the information gathered from within the school about the pupil's progress, alongside national data and expectations of progress. This should include high-quality and accurate formative assessment, using effective tools and early assessment materials. For higher levels of need, schools should have arrangements in place to draw on more specialised assessments from external agencies and professionals. This information gathering should include an early discussion with the pupil and their parents. Consideration of whether special educational provision is required should start with the desired outcomes, including the expected progress and attainment and the views and wishes of the pupil and their parents. This should then help determine the support that is needed and whether it can be provided by the school.

External factors

School staff, and this includes TAs, should also be alert to other events that can lead to learning difficulties or wider mental health difficulties, such as bullying or bereavement. Such events will not always lead to children having SEN but can have an impact, sometimes severe, on well-being. Schools should ensure they make appropriate provision for a child's short-term needs in order to prevent problems escalating. There are a number of factors or life events which can cause children to be disadvantaged. Young carers are an example of this, as are children of prisoners. A family bereavement or divorce can also affect children in the short-term.

Pupils with English as an additional language

Identifying and assessing SEN for children or young people whose first language is not English requires particular care. Difficulties related solely to limitations in English as an additional language are *not* SEN. Schools need to look carefully at all aspects of a pupil's performance in different areas of learning and development to see whether lack of progress is due to limitations in their command of English or if it arises from SEN or a disability.

Where there are long-lasting difficulties, schools should consider whether the child might have SEN. Slow progress and low attainment do not necessarily mean that a child has SEN and should not automatically lead to a pupil being recorded as having SEN as they may just be a slow learner. Equally, it should not be assumed that attainment in line with chronological age means that there is no learning difficulty or disability. Some learning difficulties and disabilities occur across the range of cognitive abilities and, left unaddressed, may lead to frustration, which may show as social, emotional or behavioural difficulties.

Does the pupil need additional support?

What can affect SEN?

The quality of teaching

The Code makes this important point:

'The quality of teaching for pupils with SEN, and the progress made by pupils, should be a core part of the school's performance management arrangements and its approach to professional development for all teaching and support staff.'

This has implications for the training and professional development of TAs as well as teachers so that pupils with SEN make good progress.

The Code states that teachers are responsible and accountable for the progress and development of the pupils in their class, including where pupils have support from TAs or specialist staff. High-quality teaching, differentiated for individual pupils, is the first step in responding to pupils who have or may have SEN. TAs are frequently used to support differentiation. Most schools review the quality of teaching regularly. This includes reviewing and, where necessary, improving, teachers' understanding of strategies to identify and support vulnerable pupils and their knowledge of the SENs most frequently encountered.

Monitoring and reviewing progress

Who should be informed?

The Code states that all teachers and support staff, usually TAs who work with pupils, should be made aware of their needs, the outcomes sought, the support provided and any teaching strategies or approaches that are required. The support and intervention provided should be selected to meet the outcomes identified for the pupil, based on reliable evidence of effectiveness, and should be provided by staff with sufficient skills and knowledge. (This has implications for TA training.) Parents should be fully aware of the planned support and interventions and, where appropriate, plans should seek parental involvement to reinforce or contribute to progress at home.

Who is responsible for pupils with SEN?

The Code states that the class or subject teacher should remain responsible for working with the child on a daily basis. Where the interventions involve group or one-to-one teaching away from the main class or subject teacher, they should still retain responsibility for the pupil. They should work closely with any *teaching assistants* or specialist staff involved, to plan and assess the impact of support and interventions and how they can be linked to classroom teaching. The SENCO should support the class or subject teacher in the further assessment of the child's particular strengths and weaknesses, in problem-solving and advising on the effective implementation of support.

When should progress be reviewed?

The effectiveness of the support and interventions and their impact on the pupil's progress should be reviewed and evaluated, along with the views of the pupil and their parents. (The TA has an important role in evaluating what works.) The class or subject teacher, working with the SENCO, should revise the support in light of the pupil's progress and development, deciding on any changes to the support and outcomes in consultation with the parent and pupil. Progress of pupils at the 'school support' stage is usually reviewed termly and sometimes twice termly in line with the school's assessment points.

Where a pupil has an EHC plan, the local authority must review that plan as a minimum every 12 months involving parents, pupils and school staff (sometimes the TA). Schools must provide an annual report for parents on their child's progress. Most schools go beyond this and provide regular reports for parents on how their child is progressing. Where a pupil is receiving SEN support, schools should talk to parents regularly to set clear outcomes and review progress towards them, discuss the activities and support that will help achieve them, and identify the responsibilities of the parent, the pupil and the school. Schools should meet parents at least three times each year. As a TA you may be asked to join these meetings and give your views. This can be daunting at first but, with support from the teacher or SENCO, you will be able to provide valuable information.

Whichever way support is provided, a clear date for reviewing progress should be agreed and the parent, pupil and teaching staff (including TAs), should each be clear about how they will help the pupil reach the expected outcomes.

'Ahem! Friends, parents and countrymen ... '

Transition arrangements

From Year 9 onwards, the programme outcomes should include those needed to make successful transitions between phases of education and to prepare for adult life. Most schools make links with secondary schools or further education (FE) providers as necessary to help plan for these transitions. Some TAs help pupils in making transitions, e.g. from nursery to infant school or indeed through any other transition by accompanying the pupil in the new setting until he or she has settled in.

Activity

Take a look at the sub-headings in this chapter and make a list of how a TA can support the SEN processes.

CHAPTER 9

Supporting children and young people with special educational needs

Chapter summary

- The Code of Practice
- Communication and interaction
  - Speech and Language difficulties
  - Dyslexia/specific learning difficulties
  - Dyspraxia
  - Autistic spectrum disorder (ASD) including autism and Asperger's syndrome
- Cognition and learning
  - Mild learning difficulties
  - Moderate learning difficulties
  - Severe learning difficulties
  - Profound and multiple learning difficulties
- Sensory and/or physical
  - Physical disability
  - Sensory impairment
  - Visual impairment (VI)
  - Hearing impairment (HI)
  - Cochlear implants
- Sensory integration disorders
- Supporting pupils with medical needs
- Activity

The Code of Practice

All teaching assistants (TAs) are very likely to come across a wide range of special educational needs in the course of their work so it is important to know what the learning implications of these needs are and how to give support.

As we saw in the last chapter, four main groups of SEN are used in the Special Educational Needs and Disability Code of Practice (2015), encompassing the full range of learning needs from 'severe' to comparatively 'mild':

- **Communication and interaction**: Many children with SEN have some degree of difficulty in at least one of the areas of speech, language and communication. These include children with speech and language difficulties, specific learning difficulties (including dyslexia and dyspraxia) and hearing impairments. Children who demonstrate features within the autistic spectrum (ASD) and those with moderate, severe or profound learning difficulties will almost certainly be included in this grouping.

- **Cognition and learning**: Included in this group are children who have moderate, severe or profound learning difficulties, or specific learning difficulties such as dyslexia or dyspraxia, and require specific programmes to aid progress in learning.

- **Social, emotional and mental health**: This group includes children who are depressed or isolated, those whose behaviour is disruptive and challenging and those who self-harm. Children who appear hyperactive and lack the ability to concentrate may also form part of this group, as will those with immature social skills.

- **Sensory and/or physical**: This group encompasses children with a wide range of sensory, multi-sensory and physical difficulties. The range extends from profound and permanent deafness or blindness to lesser levels of hearing loss or visual impairment. Sensory integration difficulties are also identified within this section. The term 'physical disability' also covers a continuum of disabling mobility and coordination difficulties.

It is important to recognise that a child's needs often overlap these groups and the key issue is meeting individual needs, regardless of which group or category they fall into. Behavioural difficulties do not necessarily mean that the child or young person has a SEN and should not automatically lead to a pupil being registered as having SEN, although some behaviours that are hard to manage are indicators of certain types of SEN, e.g. Attention Deficit Disorder (ADD). (See Chapter 10 for more on social, emotional, mental health and behavioural difficulties, including ADD.)

Communication and interaction

This category of special educational needs includes:

- speech and language difficulties
- specific learning difficulties/dyslexia

● dyspraxia

● Autistic spectrum disorder (ASD) including Asperger's syndrome

Speech and Language difficulties

Some children do not develop speech and language as expected. They may experience difficulties with any or all aspects of speech and language – from moving the muscles which control speech to the ability to understand or use language at all. These difficulties can range from the mild to the severe and long-term.

Sometimes these difficulties are unrelated to any other difficulty or disorder – they are, therefore, said to be specific language difficulties. Some children may have both a specific language difficulty and other disabilities.

Education and participation in society depend upon the ability to communicate. It is vital that children with speech and language impairments are offered comprehensive help as early as possible.

It has been estimated that there are approximately 250,000 children under five and the same number between the ages of five and sixteen in England and Wales who have language impairment. Some are in special schools but the majority attends mainstream schools (figures and information from the Association For All Speech Impaired Children, AFASIC).

If identified at a preschool level, the children will receive support from speech and language therapy services and a fortunate few attend nurseries with specially trained teachers and therapists. For some children, appropriate support in those vital early years is enough to enable them to overcome their difficulties but others go into school with an 'invisible' disability and require ongoing support from teachers, speech and language therapists and teaching assistants. Often the role of the TA is to work with the child to follow an individual programme which is monitored by the speech and language therapist and the teacher. This is likely to require a short time each day working individually or in small groups with the child. It will be helpful if you can look for ways of practising the individual activities in lessons too.

The term 'language impairment' covers a range of difficulties. It is helpful to think of these difficulties in the following ways:

Difficulties in understanding (receptive language)

● limited knowledge of vocabulary;

● difficulties in understanding meanings of words.

Difficulties in speaking (expressive language)

● range of uses for which language is employed;

● poor pronunciation;

● disordered structure of language (words omitted, in the wrong order, tense, etc.);

- limited vocabulary;

- stammering.

Different forms of speech and language impairment

- speech apparatus – the mouth, tongue, nose, breathing and how they are coordinated and operated by muscles;

- phonology – the sounds that make up language;

- syntax or grammar – the way that words and parts of words combine in phrases and sentences;

- semantics – the meaning of sentences, words, and bits of words (semantic and pragmatic disorders);

- pragmatics – how language is used in different situations and how feelings are conveyed;

- intonation and stress (prosody) – the rhythm and music of the way we speak.

Different types of difficulty require different interventions. There are many children in our schools who have delayed language development (i.e. language develops normally but at a slower rate) and who benefit from language 'enrichment' activities. This means providing new experiences and teaching the words to use alongside these experiences. Boys often develop speech and language skills at a slower rate than girls, but catch up later. Other children have disordered patterns of language development and these pupils require a more intensive approach, using the skills of speech and language therapists and specialised schemes (e.g. the Derbyshire Language Scheme, Makaton Sign System, Blissymbols, Picture Exchange Communication System: PECS).

If you are working with a child who has language impairment, it is important that you and the class teacher meet with the speech and language therapist to discuss the child's particular difficulties and how you can provide effective help. The programme can form part of the individual learning programme.

How can I give support?

- Get the child's attention before interaction. Often listening and watching are required by the child to help understanding.

- Main content words should be stressed and understanding will be helped by exaggerated intonation.

- Use simple signs or natural gestures to help the child understand your message.

- Use short, clear sentences.

- Talk about objects and activities in which the child shows an interest.

- Talk about (i.e. commentate) on actions as they are happening.

- Give the child *time* to respond. Responding in turn is a valuable skill, so try not to dominate the interaction.

- Encourage all spontaneous utterances where appropriate and help the child to feel an equal partner in conversation.

- Do not ask too many questions because they may discourage communication. Balance your talking with comment and description as well. Make up simple 'stories' using favourite toys.

- Use expansion and extension of the child's utterances. Expansion – repeat the sentence adding words that were missed out. Extension – a reply that broadens the focus of attention.

- If sounds or words are said incorrectly by the child, repeat the utterance yourself to show the correct way to say it. This is valuable feedback and should sound natural rather than like a 'correction'.

- Don't try to correct everything at once. Choose a sound, or a concept, to focus on for a week or two.

- No-one enjoys being corrected all the time. We all learn best when we feel relaxed, confident and are enjoying the task. Therefore, praise the child when his or her speech is clear, new words are attempted, or longer sentences are tried.

- Encourage the child to express him or herself through art and craft work or construction toys. (For further information visit the AFASIC website: Association for all speech impaired children, AFASIC, www.afasic.org.uk.)

Dyslexia/specific learning difficulties

Pupils described as having specific learning difficulties have average or better general ability but poor literacy skills (reading, spelling, and writing) and sometimes poor numeracy skills and concentration. There is a mis-match between the pupil's ability to understand and answer questions verbally, which is good, and the ability of the pupil to read, spell or write, which is poor. Sometimes pupils have a phonological problem which leads to specific difficulties. These sorts of problems are sometimes referred to as dyslexia. A significant number of children have specific learning difficulties which are relatively mild and more boys than girls are affected. Estimates suggest that ten in every hundred of the population may be affected, with four in every hundred having marked difficulties requiring a high level of support.

What are the learning implications?

- A limited ability to remember letter shapes and sequence.
- Difficulty learning to read or write.
- Difficulty copying from the whiteboard.
- Difficulty writing or remembering verbal instructions.

- Difficulty in planning or writing essays.

- They often have what is described as 'phonological difficulties', which is the ability to manipulate the sounds of letters into words.

- Difficulties in remembering sequences, e.g. months of the year.

- Confusion about directions, e.g. left/right.

- Loss of confidence as they realise that others can do what they can't. This sometimes results in frustration and can lead to 'playing up'.

How can I give support?

- Find out what the pupil is good at and make sure those skills are valued. Pupils who have dyslexia frequently experience feelings of frustration and loss of confidence, so it is really important that self-esteem is boosted.

- The pupil is not being lazy if he or she seems to have forgotten all the work done at the last session – or even five minutes ago! Strategies for remembering sequences and written information are poor so daily activities to improve memory can be of great value.

- Copying from the board or from textbooks may be very difficult. Give the pupil small photocopied chunks at a time or read the words to him or her and give support in encouraging writing.

- Check that the task is understood by asking the pupil to tell you what has to be done.

- Do not ask the pupil to read aloud in front of the class.

- Check that the task has been written down correctly.

- Reduce spelling lists to five words and test and retest within a short time. Early practice really helps to consolidate words in the long-term memory.

- Allow the pupil to use a Dictaphone to record ideas, e.g. in creative writing or describing a science experiment. You may then be able to transcribe the words which the child can then copy.

- Allow use of a highlighter pen to identify key words or phrases.

- Encourage the use of a laptop or word processor for recording information. The Spellchecker facility can really help to boost the confidence of these pupils.

- Use computer learning games with the pupil. These are non-judgmental so the pupil is not embarrassed by failure.

- Use a 'multi-sensory' approach to learning. This means using visual, auditory and kinesthetic (movement) strategies or clues to help them learn and remember which letter sounds and letter shapes go together.

- Some pupils report that coloured overlays are helpful and 'stop the words wobbling about', to quote one pupil.

- Many pupils confuse right and left. You can help with this by reminding them of a prompt, e.g. 'Think of which hand you normally write with, e.g. I write with my right'.

(Further help and information is available from the British Dyslexia Association: www.bda-dyslexia.org.uk.)

Dyspraxia

Dyspraxia is a label given to marked difficulties in coordination. It is described as an immaturity in the organisation of movement and may also affect language, perception and thought. A useful description is: *'Problems in getting our bodies to do what we want when we want them to do it.'* (Ripley, Daines and Barrett, 1997).

The Dyspraxia Foundation estimates that it affects at least 2 per cent of the population in varying degrees and 70 per cent of those affected are male.

Children described as dyspraxic are often described as 'clumsy'. They bump into things and fall over more often than most children and they have difficulty learning to do tasks which involve a high level of coordination such as getting dressed, writing and riding a bike.

What signs might indicate 'dyspraxic' difficulties?
The Dyspraxia Foundation lists the following possible indications of difficulty:

- clumsiness;
- poor posture, poor body awareness and awkward movement;
- confusion over handedness;
- sensitive to touch and find some clothes uncomfortable;
- poor short-term memory – can forget tasks learned that day;
- reading/writing difficulties – holding of pens can be awkward;

- poor sense of direction;
- finds it hard to catch, run, skip or use equipment;
- immature behaviour;
- poor organisational skills;
- activities requiring a sequence are difficult, e.g. maths or any subject requiring a series of tasks;
- poor awareness of time;
- easily tired;
- lack of awareness of potential danger, especially important in practical and science subjects.

Before the teacher and TA plan an individual programme for the pupil it is important to observe him or her, paying attention to the following areas:

- Gross motor skills – observation in PE will reveal if the pupil is having more difficulty than most in following action sequences. If he or she takes ages to change for PE this may also indicate coordination problems.
- Fine motor skills – observing how the pupil responds to art and craft activities (using scissors, rulers, etc.) will reveal any problem areas.
- Speech – listen to the child's pronunciation. If it is poor and the child mixes up words or sounds, then this may indicate a problem.
- Perceptual skills – observe how the child matches patterns or copies sequences of words, letters or numbers – if he or she takes ages or gets it wrong then there will be a need for support.
- Literacy and numeracy – watch how the pupil responds to the teacher, sets out written work and see whether he or she works logically. If the work is very untidy and poorly presented or there has been only patchy understanding then there will be a need for support.

How can I give support?

Pupils described as dyspraxic usually are of normal intelligence and their verbal communication can often be good. When working with a pupil described as dyspraxic it is important to remember the following guidelines:

- Break the learning task down into small steps so that each step can be mastered before moving on to the next step in the sequence.
- Practise these small steps daily, e.g. in buttoning a shirt you may need to start by showing the child where to put his fingers and how to hold the button.
- Provide written lists, e.g. the timetable, equipment necessary for particular lessons, and attach these to the child's schoolbag using luggage labels.

- Do not expect the child to copy large chunks of information from the board.

- Encourage use of word processors or laptops for recording written information.

- Ask for information given by the teacher to be repeated by the pupil (perception checking).

- Remember to boost the self-esteem of the pupil by recognising success and encouraging him or her in doing anything they can do well, e.g. singing, helping others, conversing, etc.

Occupational therapists offer help in some cases and can assess pupils. They then can recommend particular equipment or approaches. Where difficulties severely affect a pupil's progress in school, referral to the occupational therapist for further assessment is crucial. The occupational therapist may treat the pupil's problems directly and/or set up a programme in school (with advice to the family at home). Such programmes are often carried out by the TA who is trained by the occupational therapist to work with the individual child; monitoring and reviewing are carried out on a regular basis. Advice on management and equipment will also be given.

If you want to know more about dyspraxia then the following resources are useful:

- www.dyspraxiafoundation.org.uk
- *Dyspraxia, a Guide for Teachers and Parents* by Kate Ripley, Bob Daines and Jenny Barrett (David Fulton Publishers)

Autistic spectrum disorder (ASD) including autism and Asperger's syndrome

Many pupils with special needs have difficulties communicating effectively as a result of a learning difficulty or physical or sensory impairment. However, there are a small number of pupils whose major problem is an inability to communicate with and make sense of the world around them. These children have a normal physical appearance and can hear and see but they fail to understand the meaning of language and of social situations. Some of them seem to lack the desire to communicate socially. Children and young people having this kind of difficulty sometimes have a medical diagnosis of autism, or, if they are more able, of Asperger's syndrome. These difficulties come under the umbrella term of autistic spectrum disorders (ASD). ASD is a generic term used to describe people who have a common set of difficulties that affect communication, relationships and imagination. Individuals with ASD range from those with severe learning difficulties to those with high intelligence.

ASDs are relatively rare and those pupils with severe learning difficulties are educated in special schools More able pupils, with Asperger's syndrome, can usually cope with the demands of mainstream schools but only when supported effectively by the school and teaching assistants. Some mainstream schools have special units for pupils with ASD.

ASD is a generic term used to describe people who have a common set of difficulties that affect communication, relationships and imagination. ASD results in difficulties in three areas of development.

Social interaction

Pupils with ASD can display a marked aloofness and indifference to other people, a passive acceptance of social contact or an inappropriately stilted and formal manner of interaction, not being able to modify their tone of voice. They seem odd or eccentric and are unable to show empathy with others or interpret emotions.

Social communication

Pupils with ASD range from not speaking or communicating at all, either by word or action, through to understanding words but not being able to understand the hidden rules of normal conversation or the nuances of meaning, e.g. jokes. They frequently take things literally, e.g. 'Pull your socks up'.

Imagination

Some pupils may show bizarre or sometimes obsessive interest in facts and figures, such as timetables or road networks. They find it difficult to engage in social or imaginative play.

Some of the special characteristics associated with this difficulty include anxiety as some situations and instructions appear confusing. Sometimes they react to situations by using stereotyped behaviour such as rocking or twiddling.

What are the learning implications?

- Pupils need to be taught social and communication skills.
- Children frequently take things literally and this can cause anxiety.
- The pupil will not respond as others do, they will not seek contact or take part in activities as others do.
- They need routines and become anxious when routines are changed.
- It is sometimes hard to know how much the pupil understands.
- Sometimes the child may have unfounded but genuine fears about certain objects, animals or people.
- Some may dislike the noise and disorder of break-times.

How can I give support?

- Explain statements and instructions carefully using words, actions, pictures or role-play to help the child's understanding of the situation.
- Accompany the pupil in the playground if the playground causes anxiety.
- Children need help to know *how* to behave in social situations. Model or teach them what is expected and to encourage appropriate behaviour.

- Children tend to withdraw when they cannot make sense of what is going on. You need to *anticipate* what will cause anxiety and make changes accordingly.

- Prepare the child for what is going to happen next, by talking him or her through the situation. Written instructions, timetables and timelines help a lot.

- Physical activity (e.g. jogging, ball play) can be helpful in reducing anxiety and physical tension. Music and relaxation techniques will help.

- Do give praise and encouragement. Even though it may not seem to be received, these pupils need positive feedback and reassurance.

- Encourage friendships and group work, enabling other pupils to understand ASD.

- Be careful in your use of facial expression. Some children get anxious if they feel you are cross with them; this may result in difficult behaviour.

It is important to note that children who have the same diagnosis of ASD can have significantly differing needs. All children are individuals and their specific needs must be considered and addressed.

(More information about children with ASD is provided by the National Autistic Society: www.nas.org.uk.)

The book *The Curious Incident of the Dog in the Night-Time* is written by Mark Haddon, who has Asperger's syndrome, and this provides some interesting insights into his perceptions.

Cognition and learning

This group of special educational needs includes:

- mild learning difficulties;
- moderate learning difficulties;
- severe learning difficulties;
- profound and multiple learning difficulties.

Mild learning difficulties

It has been estimated that 18 per cent of all pupils will have some kind of mild learning difficulty at some time during their school life. Most pupils are educated in mainstream schools and are likely to be supported in the category of 'school support'. Some pupils may only need additional support for a short period as they may catch up with their peers. Teaching assistants are frequently called upon to support such pupils whose mild special needs may be any of the following:

- mild conductive hearing loss (e.g. 'glue ear');
- slight physical disability (e.g. mild cerebral palsy);

- poor eye/hand coordination;
- clumsiness;
- hyperactivity;
- slow to develop reading and writing skills;
- general immaturity;
- poor vocabulary;
- slow to understand new ideas;
- short concentration span/distractibility.

These pupils should not need a high level of support but attention needs to be given to particular areas of need with the possibility of including structured activities to support the particular need.

The vast majority of children who have mild learning difficulties lack self-confidence in their learning ability. Please remember to take every opportunity to enable the child to succeed and be ready to give praise and encouragement for small amounts of progress. What appears to be a small step may be a giant leap for the child.

Moderate learning difficulties

Pupils described as having moderate learning difficulties (MLD) are often pupils who have limited ability in both verbal and non-verbal skills. They are pupils who learn at a slower pace than do other boys and girls of the same age.

It used to be the case that pupils identified with MLD were educated in special schools. Since the 1981 Education Act and its emphasis on children being educated in the mainstream where possible, increasing numbers of pupils with MLD have their needs met in ordinary schools, usually with additional teacher support and/or teaching assistance. The main indicator of whether this is in the best interests of the pupil is the ability of the pupil to cope with the social and emotional demands of a mainstream school setting, and the ability of the mainstream school to provide an appropriate curriculum and welcoming ethos. There may remain a number of such pupils who require the more sheltered and nurturing support which special schools offer and who would struggle to cope and fail to thrive in a mainstream setting. It is possible to replicate more 'sheltered and nurturing' environments in mainstream schools where resources are available.

Pupils who have moderate learning difficulties often have the following associated problems:

- poor memory;
- short attention span;
- slow progress in literacy and numeracy skills;
- limited ability to apply learning in one situation to another situation (generalisation);
- inability to understand abstract ideas.

If you are working with a pupil who is described as having moderate learning difficulties, please remember:

- He or she needs practical work in order to learn ('active learning'). Every opportunity for using visual aids and practical apparatus should be used.

- *Overlearning is necessary.*

  Frequent repetition and practice of skills acquired is important in order to reinforce learning.

- *Language work is essential.*

  Vocabulary and language use is likely to be poor, so regular activities which broaden vocabulary and increase understanding of language are essential.

- *Progress in literacy and numeracy will be slow.*

  The class teacher and SENCO will help you to understand how best to support children in learning to read, spell, write and do number work.

- *Confidence building is crucial.*

  Children described as having moderate learning difficulties often have low self-esteem and perceive themselves as failures, so take every opportunity to give praise and build confidence.

- *Lift skills will need to be taught.*

  Young people who are described as having moderate learning difficulties need help to learn those skills they will need when they leave school, e.g. filling in forms, managing their money, relationship issues etc.

Severe learning difficulties

Pupils described as having severe learning difficulties are usually pupils who have very limited general ability and who learn at a much slower pace than other boys and girls of the same age. These learning difficulties are often because these children are genetically different from most other children, e.g. Down's syndrome, or they have experienced a medical trauma, e.g. brain damage as a result of tumour or oxygen deprivation at birth. Most pupils are educated in special schools although some are wholly or partially integrated in mainstream schools with the teaching resources they require.

Pupils who are described as having severe learning difficulties have similar characteristics to those with moderate difficulties but they frequently need a higher level of adult support and learn at a slower rate. Even as adults, some may be unable to cope independently without the support of caring adults. It is therefore necessary to teach life skills (shopping, cooking) to the pupils as a priority, particularly as they get older. The younger child will take longer to learn 'self-help' skills (e.g. feeding, use of toilet) and your help is likely in these areas.

If you are working with a child who has severe learning difficulties, please remember:

- *Slow progress is likely.*

  Progress may be slow but the children can and do learn given consistent support at the right level.

- *Practical experiences are vital.*

  The need for 'first-hand' experience is clear (e.g. shopping trips to learn about the use of money).

- *Language work is essential.*

  Encouraging understanding of language and use of language is very important in the learning process.

- *Allow the pupil to choose.*

  Try to provide the pupil with opportunities to make choices, as it is by developing the ability to choose that control over the environment is developed. Don't let the pupil become too dependent on you!

Profound and multiple learning difficulties

Pupils described as having profound and multiple learning difficulties (PMLD) have both severe physical disabilities and severe learning difficulties. They may also have sensory impairment (hearing and sight). They often have limited understanding of language and little or no speech, so communication is often difficult.

When working with children who have PMLD, most of whom are educated in special schools, the first priority must be their physical comfort. There will be many routine tasks (feeding, dressing, toileting) which they cannot do for themselves and your help will be required. In order to assist with some of these tasks you will need clear directions on how to move pupils from one place to another, both for their comfort and your own. Backache is a common complaint among adults who work with children because of the lifting involved. Do ask about how you can avoid this and learn the correct techniques for lifting and moving children.

Once the child is comfortable, the priorities then become educational. Establishing some means of communication is of key importance. This may be through visual contact, through touch, through sounds, through taste and smell, i.e. working through all the senses.

If you are working with a child who has profound and multiple learning difficulties, please remember:

- Children and young people with PMLD can and do learn, although progress is often very slow.

- Try to understand what messages the child's behaviour may be communicating.

● Have positive expectations.

● Give encouragement and praise even though you may be unsure of whether the child understands. Assume that he or she does. If you seem to get no response, it may be because the child cannot physically make the response – there may be a response which you cannot see.

● In some cases, children will actually regress as a result of medical factors and occasionally a child may die. Be aware that this is a possibility. You may be included in support for the family or for other pupils if this happens.

Sensory and/or physical

This group of special educational needs includes:

● hearing impairment or deafness (HI)

● visual impairment (VI)

● multi-sensory impairment (MSI)

● physical disabilities (PD)

● sensory integration disorders (SID)

Physical disability

The term physical disability covers a wide range of conditions. The more common ones you are likely to come across include:

● cerebral palsy	● epilepsy
● spina bifida	● haemophilia
● hydrocephalus	● limb deficiency
● cystic fibrosis	● asthma
● muscular dystrophy	● brittle bone disease
● diabetes	● eczema

Within each category, the effects of the disability range from the relatively minor, so that the child can lead a 'normal' independent life, to relatively severe, so that the child cannot function without the support of caring adults.

Until quite recently, pupils with physical disabilities attended special schools, but ideas about physical disabilities have changed from the rather negative concept of 'handicap' to the more positive concepts of 'disability' or 'impairment'. The rights of people with disabilities to have access to normal experiences have been recognised and the general public is much more aware of people with disabilities and the part they play in community life. Whenever possible, these pupils should have their needs met in mainstream schools. There are still a considerable number of children whose additional needs are such that special schooling is appropriate at present. This will be when the pupil's health is at risk, and/or they require very specialised equipment and/or daily intensive physiotherapy, i.e. those who would 'fail to thrive' in a mainstream setting either physically or emotionally.

Different disabilities result in different learning support needs. You will need to ask the teacher you work with about the details of the disability – educational psychologists, teacher advisers and school medical officers (doctors) can also give you details of associated learning difficulties and physical needs. For instance, pupils who have cerebral palsy sometimes have visuo-perceptual difficulties, i.e. they do not perceive visual images in the same way as other children. Pupils with hydrocephalus sometimes have mood swings and experience times when they feel very tired. Pupils with spina bifida sometimes have poor fine motor control (i.e. poor control of pencil and hand movements).

On the other hand, it is likely that pupils with cystic fibrosis, asthma or brittle bone disease may have no learning difficulties as such but they may need a sensitivity to other needs, e.g. tiredness, mood swings, and assistance in managing equipment or physiotherapy routines.

One step behind/promoting independence

Promoting independence is an essential part of your role with all pupils who need learning support. It is particularly important for pupils who have physical disabilities. You need to be 'one step behind' rather than 'one step ahead'. This means allowing the pupil to take calculated risks, on occasion – you will need to discuss this with the class teacher, head teacher, teacher adviser and on occasions the school medical officer, and think through the possible consequences.

Perhaps the hardest task that TAs face in supporting this group of children and young people is that of maintaining the balance between giving support and promoting independence. There is a danger that the pupil will become much too dependent on you if you do too much for them. You will need to be clear about your expectations and firm in your directions without pressurising the child. However, sensitivity should tell you if and when to intervene.

Self-help

Part of your role may be enabling the child to look after himself or herself and to master those skills which able-bodied children take for granted, e.g. feeding, dressing, going to the toilet. When helping children in these ways it is important to treat them with dignity and respect and to provide privacy when appropriate.

Mobility

Pupils may need aids in the form of wheelchairs, crutches, mechanical limbs or calipers in order to get around. You will need to familiarise yourself with this equipment and make sure the pupil can use it with comfort and control. Most children learn to transfer themselves from place to place when required, e.g. from a wheelchair to the toilet, with little help. Younger children or very disabled pupils may need more help. If you need to assist in moving a child, you must know the correct techniques for lifting in order to avoid injury to either yourself or the child. Ask for support – quite literally! Lifting techniques must be taught, for each child, by a physiotherapist.

When working with a child with a physical disability, please remember:

- Behave towards him or her as you would to any other pupil of the same age.

- Do not do all the talking for the child or answer for him or her. Let the child make choices so he or she feels they have some control of their environment rather than becoming a passive recipient of support.

- Give him or her the *time* to make a response – they may take longer to respond than others. Often their thinking response is immediate but controlling arms and legs, voice or equipment to aid communication can take time.

- Make sure you know the implications of the disability (physical, educational and emotional).

If you want to know more about physical disability, the SCOPE website is useful: www.scope.org.uk.

Sensory impairment

Sensory impairment, as the name suggests, refers to any impairment of the senses which may prevent normal progress and development. There are two main types, visual impairment (VI) and hearing impairment (HI). Rarely, children will have both.

Visual impairment (VI)

A survey by the Royal National Institute for the Blind (2014) indicated that in Britain there were 25,294 children and young people supported by visual impairment services. This number includes those in mainstream schools and units and those in special schools who may have additional learning difficulties. The survey also found that there were 2,431 TAs employed to support them.

This survey also showed the increase over recent years in the proportion of VI children who go to mainstream schools with varying levels of support; a lot of this support comes from teaching assistants together with peripatetic teachers of the visually impaired.

> *'Participation of disabled children in inclusive education is now well established in policy and practice.'*
>
> *(RNIB survey 2014)*

The impairment may be moderate, in which case your work might be mainly concerned with adapting materials and ensuring safety. If the impairment is severe you may need to learn Braille and keyboard skills in order to produce materials the pupil can use and thus learn effectively. You may also need to assist the pupil in learning how to get around the classroom and school with safety. It is important to understand the limits of the pupil's vision.

When working with a visually impaired pupil, your responsibilities are likely to be as follows:

- to provide support for the class teacher by adapting teaching materials, e.g. enlarging worksheets, so that the pupil can follow the same programmes of work as the other members of the class;
- you may be asked to supervise the specialist equipment and resources, e.g. magnifying equipment;
- to ensure the safety of the pupil and others, e.g. safe use of science equipment;
- to support the pupil by helping him or her to learn any special skills, e.g. Braille;
- to work under the guidance of teachers who provide specialist support for VI pupils.

You will need to offer support in all areas in which he or she may be disadvantaged. These areas are:

Orientation and mobility

Clear verbal directions are necessary before any task involving physical movement is attempted. The visually impaired child may not have a visual image of what is required so a visual demonstration is a waste of time, e.g. in PE, if the class teacher is demonstrating, you may need to talk through the steps, for instance, 'Move three steps to the right, jump with both feet together, then three steps to the left'.

Environmental awareness

Visually impaired children must be helped to become aware of their surroundings and learn how to cope with a range of situations, both inside and outside. Schools can help by making adaptations to help pupils get around the site, e.g. hand rails, brightly coloured strips on steps, etc.

Games and leisure

It is sometimes difficult for children with sight problems to join in with informal games and conversations. You may be able to help here by opening up possibilities for the child you work with to join in and become part of the group.

Social skills

The child with a visual impairment has a social communication problem as he or she cannot always see and therefore interpret the intentions of others.

A major way in which children learn is through copying other children and adults, but a child with a visual impairment may be unable to do this. This means that he or she will be unable to see a great many actions, facial expressions and non-verbal messages and, as a result, may miss out on this type of learning. Don't be offended if the child uses the wrong non-verbal messages and be prepared to teach them the acceptable ways of interacting in a group situation (e.g. remind the child to turn his or her face towards you when speaking). Some playground supervision may be necessary and your role might be to encourage inclusion of the child in group activities as far as possible.

...and remember...

Visually impaired children often miss out on ideas and meanings because of limited vision. It is therefore important to use 'hands on' experience whenever possible, e.g. when talking about leaves, give the child some leaves to hold or, better still, take the child to a park and let him or her feel a tree and walk through fallen leaves to hear the noise that makes.

If you want to know more about visual impairment and blindness, then the following resources are useful:

● Royal National Institute for the Blind website: www.rnib.org

● www.actionforblindpeople.org

● www.learninghub.royalblind.org

Hearing impairment (HI)

There is a wide range of hearing impairments, from mild to profound, although total lack of hearing is extremely rare. Statistics published by the National Deaf Children's Society estimate that there are 40,614 children and young people who are deaf or have significant hearing impairment. 85 per cent are educated in mainstream schools, an increase over the last ten years. Fifteen per cent are either in units attached to mainstream schools or in special schools for the deaf. Some children receive support from a peripatetic teacher of the hearing impaired. Over 750 TAs support these children by working with the class teacher and following specialist advice which allows the pupil to play as full a part as possible in school life.

Children and young people who have normal hearing skills acquire ideas and concepts about the world around them largely through spoken language. The words we use to describe objects and experiences provide the child with a 'framework' to build on and learn effectively from through reasoning and memory skills. For the child with a hearing impairment, understanding of language is limited, so this 'framework', which is vital for learning, is incomplete. These children may then appear slow to learn, particularly in language-based tasks of speaking, listening, reading and writing. Reasoning and memory skills may also appear to be poor. However, many of these pupils have normal ability and good non-verbal and visual skills and most acquire spoken language in the same way as hearing children but at a slower rate. There are many factors which influence whether a hearing impaired child hears and understands speech. These include:

- the kind and degree of hearing loss;
- the age at which deafness developed;
- the age at which it was discovered;
- the issue and proper use of a suitable hearing-aid;
- early training;
- attentiveness of the child.

(Bennett 1985)

As a TA working with the pupil you may find it helpful to be clear about these factors in his or her background in order to understand the hearing loss and its educational implications. Ask the specialist teacher of the hearing impaired to discuss this with you.

If you support a pupil with a hearing impairment then you need to appreciate that he or she has a *communication* problem and that your first task is to ensure as far as possible that the pupil is reliably receiving and understanding all communication from staff and other pupils and is routinely participating in all class activities. Your role with the pupil who has a moderate to profound loss might involve ensuring the correct use of any hearing-aid equipment provided and you may also need to learn a signing system if that is advised as appropriate, although relatively few children use signing in mainstream schools.

Your role with the pupil who has a hearing loss will involve ensuring that he or she is in the best position in the class to hear what the teacher says and you will need to check, by asking, whether he or she has understood the learning activity.

When working with a child or young person with hearing impairment, please remember:

- The sense of hearing is limited so reinforce as much spoken language as possible through the other senses. Visual clues through lip-reading, signing or natural gestures may be necessary to ensure that the child understands. You can be advised about this by a teacher of the hearing impaired.

- Pupils with moderate to profound hearing loss may be unable to acquire the skills of speaking, listening, reading and writing at a normal rate. For these children it is essential to provide individual programmes to focus on the development of these skills. For these pupils, appropriate activities and/or modifications to the curriculum may be advised by a specialist teacher who will discuss your role in implementing these with you and the class teacher.

- Use visual aids and real experiences whenever you can.

- Communicating with others is a basic need. Pupils with hearing impairment may feel frustrated about their inability to communicate and so may lack self-esteem and occasionally become aggressive. You will need to establish communication with the child yourself, and help others to do so. You may also need to be particularly sensitive to the child's emotional needs.

- Rephrase, reiterate and extend your language whenever possible to give the pupil with a hearing impairment a better understanding of difficult concepts. Be creative!

- Be aware of social isolation and try to foster friendships and inclusion of the pupil with the peer group.

- Hearing-aids and radio systems are the pupil's link with the sounds around him or her. Learn how the systems work and how to monitor the development of listening skills.

Cochlear implants

You may come across pupils who have cochlear implants. Cochlear implants are used more frequently than in the past to aid hearing in children who have moderate to profound hearing loss in both ears. A cochlear implant is an electronic medical device that replaces the function of the damaged inner ear. Unlike hearing aids, which make sounds louder, cochlear implants do the work of damaged parts of the inner ear (cochlea) to provide sound signals to the brain. Many children and young people have cochlear implants in both ears (bilateral). Listening with two ears can improve ability to identify the direction of sound and separate the sounds you want to hear from those you don't.

If you want to know more about deafness and hearing impairment then the following resources are useful:

- National Deaf Children's Society: NDCF www.ndcf.org

- Supporting Children with Hearing Impairment in Mainstream Schools INPUT

Sensory integration disorders

Children with profound learning difficulties sometimes have problems with sensory integration. Sensory Integration is an individual's ability to appropriately register, process and respond to a range of sensory stimulus from the sensory channels, i.e. tactile, auditory, gustatory (food texture and taste), olfactory (smell) and visual.

Sensory information is received from inside and outside the body. Some individuals may be hypo-sensitive to sensory sensation which may lead to sensory seeking behaviours whereas others may be hyper-sensitive, which may lead to defensive and avoidant behaviours. Sensory seeking behaviours may include extra touching of particular textures, excessive body movements, (rocking, twisting, stretching), chewing clothes and/or mouthing objects excessively. Sensory avoidant behaviours may include distress with loud noises, easily distracted by noise and visual stimuli, avoiding particular textures including eating some foods. Occupational therapists have a range of tests they can administer to give an indication of a child's responses relative to others of the same age. If difficulties are established, a sensory 'diet' may be advised to support the child at school. This will include specific support for the individual child/young person, often provided by a teaching assistant.

Supporting pupils with medical needs

The Children and Families Act 2014 places a duty on schools and academies to make arrangements to support pupils with medical conditions. *Individual healthcare plans* will normally specify the type and level of support required to meet the medical needs of such pupils. Where children and young people also have SEN, their provision should be planned and delivered in a coordinated way with the healthcare plan. Schools are required to have regard to statutory guidance, 'Supporting pupils at school with medical conditions' (Department for Education. Sept 2014).

There is a range of medical and neurological conditions which you may be asked to support, ranging from fairly common conditions like eczema and asthma to more complex conditions like epilepsy or cystic fibrosis. There are also allergies, e.g. peanut allergy, which you will need to know about and react to if a problem arises. As an assistant, you may have a role in administering medication, under the direction of the teacher or school nurse, or delivering specific physiotherapy or speech therapy programmes. If you are working with a pupil who has epileptic episodes, you will need to know how to deal with this, for example, how to respond to a fit. The school nurse will be able to give you the information needed to support medical conditions and you will find it useful to talk with the child's parents about the implications. You will need to know how to respond in the case of any emergency. If you are not sure, then do ask.

Activity

Think of a pupil in your school who has one or more of the special educational needs described in this chapter.

- Take a look at the recommendations for support and list the strategies you are already using and then the strategies you have not yet tried.

- Make a plan to try these different strategies.

CHAPTER 10

Supporting social, emotional, behavioural and mental health needs

Chapter summary

- Social, emotional and mental health difficulties (SEMH)
  - What do we mean by 'social, emotional and mental health difficulties'?
  - How common are mental health difficulties?
  - What mental health difficulties do I need to be aware of?
  - What can I do about it?
  - Some key ideas in supporting children who have social, emotional or mental health difficulties
- Behaviour difficulties
  - What 'problem' behaviours will I see in the classroom?
  - How can I prevent problems occurring?
  - Supporting pupils with behaviour difficulties
  - Planning a structured behaviour programme for an individual pupil
- Attention Deficit Disorder
- Activity

In the course of your work as a teaching assistant (TA) you will come across a considerable number of children and young people who need support because of social, emotional or mental health difficulties (SEMH). In recent discussions with experienced TAs, they report that children and young people seem more anxious and stressed than was the case ten years ago. They put this down to two main factors. Firstly, the mounting pressure to succeed in national tests and exams, and secondly, the increasing incidence of family breakdown and its impact on children and young people. An important part of every TA's role is noticing when pupils are struggling, and giving pupils more time as well as practical and emotional support.

The 1981 Education Act recognised that emotional and behavioural needs are special *educational* needs because no child can learn optimally if they are unsettled or unhappy in school for whatever reason. Sometimes these difficulties are caused as a result of physical, sensory or learning disabilities but often they are rooted in difficult home backgrounds. There is usually a combination of factors which come together to cause the child to exhibit signs of social, emotional or behavioural difficulty.

What do we mean by 'social, emotional and mental health difficulties'?

Social, emotional and mental health difficulties (SEMH) is a blanket term which includes a very wide range of conditions – perhaps the only characteristic they share in common is that the children and young people experiencing them are both troubled and troubling to those who come into contact with them.

The emotional difficulties which lead to interpersonal and social problems range from, on the one hand, 'internalising' behaviour, e.g. withdrawal/shyness, depression, extreme anxiety and compulsions, to 'acting out' behaviours (sometimes called conduct disorders), e.g. extreme aggression (to people or property), anti-social behaviour, bullying, defiance.

If a child receives inadequate emotional nurturing from the parents or carers, particularly at an early age, then the likelihood of social, emotional and behavioural difficulties is high. Physical and sexual abuse also increases the likelihood of social, emotional and mental health needs.

Learning difficulties can also cause emotional or behavioural problems for children. This is particularly the case at the secondary stage when pupils become more aware of their own inability to cope well with literacy tasks. A sensitive educational environment and a curriculum at the right level and content is necessary.

There are many factors which indicate difficulties of this kind and the vast majority of children and young people, at some point in their school lives, will have some social, emotional or behavioural problems – indeed it is part of normal development. Pupils with special needs of any kind often experience these difficulties as part of their perception of themselves as being 'different'. However, it is when problems persist over a long period of time and become severe and complex that they are viewed as special educational needs. It is at this stage that additional support is needed.

Pupils experiencing severe and protracted social, emotional and behavioural difficulties may need special provision in special schools or Pupil Referral Units (PRUs) where small class groups and high levels of adult attention are provided. There are many pupils in our mainstream schools who also show these difficulties and schools report increasing numbers. Some primary schools have 'nurture groups' for children to join for part of the school day. These are smaller groupings offering more individual attention and often ensuring that the children have basic needs met, e.g. food and warm clothing as well as social and emotional support activities.

TAs play a significant part in supporting children and young people with SEMH difficulties, thus enabling them to remain in their local schools. The majority of children with SEMH difficulties do not achieve what they are capable of in academic subjects at school because no child can learn effectively if he or she is troubled inside and has feelings of worthlessness. As mentioned, some pupils react to their environment by 'acting out'. This can range from persistent bullying to anti-social acts, either in or out of school, e.g. fighting, stealing, graffiti, etc. Other pupils turn inwards and show signs of mental health problems.

How common are mental health difficulties?

UNICEF has placed the UK at number 16 in a league table of child well-being in 29 of the world's richest countries (UNICEF, 2013). This suggests that many children and young people in the UK are not as happy or contented with their life as they should be. The Health Behaviour of School-Aged Children Survey (2009–10) (HBCS) found that around 30 per cent of English adolescents reported a level of emotional well-being considered as (sub-clinical) 'low grade' poor mental health, that is they regularly (at least once a week) feel low, sad or down. This is higher among girls than boys.

In a study of pupils considered to be 'at risk' of exclusion from their secondary schools, all had recent or current traumas in their home life; 75 per cent had poor reading skills and 25 per cent were identified as having quite marked signs of mental health problems (anorexia, bulimia, self-harm, etc.). Research from the Tavistock Clinic in London indicates that 75 per cent of all adult mental illness is evident before the age of 18, and one in ten pupils have a mental health disorder at some stage (ref; Mending Young Minds. BBC Radio 4 Nov 2015).

A statement from the mental health charity Young Minds says:

> *'Young people today are growing up in a harsh environment with ever increasing stress to perform at school, next to zero job prospects and the constant pressure to keep up with the latest consumer trends. Social networking although creating ever greater circles of "friends" often leaves young people feeling even more isolated and alone.'*

and…

> *'Everyone should take responsibility for the next generation if we don't want these projected figures to become a reality. Parents need the tools to give their children the necessary support, schools need to place much more emphasis on teaching emotional resilience and coping skills and services that intervene early when mental health problems first arise need to be given much greater priority and appropriate investment.'*

Available data suggests that self-harm is a big issue in England. Over the last ten years there has been a 68 per cent increase in the number of young people being admitted to hospital because of self-harm, which is seen as a reaction to not coping (Young Minds, 2011). A study in 2013 found that the incidence of eating disorders in young people is also increasing.

The Understanding Society survey results for 2011–12 suggest 85.5 per cent of children belong to a social networking site. In England, the proportion of young people playing computer games for two hours or more a night during the week increased from 42 to 55 per cent among boys and 14 to 20 per cent among girls, between 2006 and 2010. The same survey suggests 12.1 per cent of children have been bullied four or more times in the last six months. In some areas more than 10 per cent of children reported being bullied. Data from the Tellus survey stated that one-third of pupils do not think their school is managing the problem well. The charity ChildLine has reported an 87 per cent rise in contacts related to online, cyber-bullying.

What mental health difficulties do I need to be aware of?

TAs often work quite closely with young people with mental health or behavioural difficulties. Young people often have mood swings and most children have temper tantrums at some stage. This is part of normal development and should not be associated with mental health problems. If you are a parent, you will be aware of this. As a TA, you will need to be alert to spotting signs of mental ill-health or changes in normal patterns of behaviour.

Self-harm: You may notice scars or wounds on wrists or forearms. Often, the pupil will try to cover these scars but you should report this if you see it.

Eating disorders (anorexia or bulimia): You may notice loss of weight or low energy, mostly in girls but boys can also be affected. Some young people who eat a lot of junk food are deficient in some vital vitamins and minerals, especially iron, so are likely to become tired towards the end of the school day. While this is not an eating disorder it is something which can affect learning and concentration. Over-eating can be a sign of depression, insecurity or other mental health difficulties.

Depression: You may notice withdrawn behaviour and isolation. Some children are naturally quiet but when you see children reluctant to participate in activities or seeming unhappy for longer periods then this will ring alarm bells. You can try to talk to the pupil using the listening skills mentioned in Chapter 3 but it is likely that he or she will need professional help.

Anxiety: There is considerable evidence that rates of anxiety have increased over recent times. This can affect teenagers in particular and can result from fearing failure in exams and being a perfectionist in life in general. The Radio 4 programme *All in the Mind* has some interesting information about the levels of anxiety in teenagers and how it affects them in everyday life. The pressure of competition and needing to succeed can lead to significant difficulties for some children and young people.

The first thing to do is to report any concerns to the teacher and SENCO who will then contact parents and other agencies who can provide skilled support. You can make additional efforts to support pupils by giving positive attention when you can. Helping them to realise that they don't need to be perfect and increasing the importance of being an individual can be helpful for children and young people. Valuing children and young people for who they are is an important step in helping them to feel that they belong and accepting who they are, irrespective of their academic or sporting achievements.

Behaviour difficulties

In your work as a TA you will become aware of a range of 'problem' behaviours in the classroom. These will range from mild 'low-level' disruptions such as pencil-tapping or social chat to full-blown tantrums or defiance. Assistants have noted the following behaviours as those causing concern:

Low level disruptions

- pencil-tapping;
- humming;
- kicking the table legs;
- chair-rocking;
- taking others' equipment;
- poking, pushing, 'interfering' with others;
- constant talking, giggling;
- fidgeting.

More serious disruptions

- shouting out;
- out of seat a lot;
- lashing out at others;
- swearing or shouting;
- defiance;
- throwing equipment;
- damaging equipment or property;
- spitting;
- bullying;
- withdrawn behaviour;
- frequent crying;
- running away;
- hiding;
- stealing.

What can I do about it?

What 'problem' behaviours will I see in the classroom?

It is important to note that most classrooms are well-managed by teachers and most behaviour problems are of the 'low-level' type, which are not a result of mental health difficulties requiring long-term support. It is rare to have major outbursts or fighting in class but if it does happen it is the responsibility of the teacher to react appropriately. If you are working with a particularly difficult pupil then you need to sit down with the teacher and plan who will do what if a major problem should occur and, more importantly, what strategies you should adopt to stop the difficult behaviours from arising. Most schools have a policy for physical restraint. Although incidents are rare, you will find it helpful to read the policy if your role incudes supporting pupils with these difficulties so that you know how to react. In general, TAs should not get involved in physical restraint unless authorised and trained by the Senior Management Team.

How can I prevent problems occurring?

In order to prevent problems occurring and to stop escalation of incidents it is important to do some analysis of just what causes the difficult behaviour in the first place. Of course, you cannot do anything about the pupil's home life but you may be able to identify when a 'difficult' day is in prospect by judging the mood of the pupil first thing in the morning. In this case you will need all your best 'active listening' skills to encourage him or her to talk about what might be troubling them. You may be able to provide some quiet time away from the class group for the pupil to 'settle' before going into lessons.

You can also prevent difficulties arising in the first place by following some of these suggestions:

- sit the pupil next to a well-behaved pupil – sitting him or her next to a 'sworn enemy' is a recipe for disaster;
- ensure he or she is sitting near the front of the class with few obstacles to pass on the way to his or her seat;
- ensure he or she has all the equipment needed;
- give the pupil tasks and activities which he or she can do – too difficult a task can cause frustration, which may lead to disruptive behaviour;
- give the pupil 'positive' attention early on in the day. Children who are 'attention-needing' are going to get your attention one way or another – usually this is through the 'negative' attention of being 'told off'. However, if you are proactive in this process and give praise and attention to the pupil *before* things start to go wrong, then you are more likely to prevent difficulties arising.

Some key ideas in supporting children who have social, emotional or mental health difficulties

Take every opportunity to improve the self-esteem of the pupil
Give praise when they conform to normally expected standards of behaviour in school or when they have achieved something they have never

done before. This can be related to school work or to behaviour. Try to 'catch them being good' and let them know why you are pleased.

> 'Jenny, I like the way you came into the classroom this morning.' (behaviour)

> 'Robert, you've read those words really well today. Well done!' (school work)

All children and young people seek to belong to the group and their self-esteem can be badly damaged if they are excluded by other members of the class. As a TA you need to foster peer group acceptance of the child so that he or she is not left out.

Work out what the pupil is communicating through their behaviour

It helps in knowing how to respond if you can work out what the pupil is trying to achieve or communicate through their disruptive behaviour. If you can identify what this is then you will be able to respond in a way which is more likely to be successful; for example, the pupil may be described as 'attention seeking'. This behaviour often irritates teachers or assistants. If you can re-frame this concept to 'attention needing', it will help. You can predict that the pupil will get the teacher's attention by being disruptive, so try giving proactive, positive attention to the pupil early on in the lesson so that he or she does not need to get the negative attention through bad behaviour.

The pupil may challenge authority. This is 'power-seeking' behaviour and arouses anger in teachers or assistants. You can respond to this by staying calm and considering how the pupil might be given some 'power' but in a positive way, e.g. some responsibility in class. Being listened to can go a long way in resolving issues.

Rewards and encouragement are very important

This shows the pupil when he or she is succeeding and that it is worth-while to succeed. Find out what the pupils you work with value as a reward. Sometimes a word of praise or a pat on the back can be enough, but for many children described as having social, emotional and behavioural difficulties, this will not be enough and you will need to provide more tangible rewards (a wall chart with targets, a favourite game, etc.). Remember the 'Goldilocks' principle … give three times as many positive comments as negative … this strategy works well although research has shown that some teachers do the reverse.

Develop your listening skills (see Chapter 3, 'Supporting the pupil')

You will be sensitive to the feelings of the pupil if you can listen and observe effectively. If you can encourage the pupil to talk about their feelings, it can be helpful. Try to look for solutions to the problems rather than dwelling on the causes. Ask what needs to happen in order to avoid this situation in the future. Try to identify the patterns of behaviour and circumstances when the unwanted behaviour does not occur. There will be many parts of the pupil's life which you cannot change for the better. Accept this and concentrate on those parts you can change (e.g. self-esteem, attitude to learning, patterns of behaviour in school).

Encourage the pupil to take responsibility

Many pupils with social, emotional and behavioural difficulties find it very hard to take responsibility for their own actions. Enabling them to understand what effects their behaviour has on others is an important step in moving towards changing unhelpful behaviour patterns. Role-play or drama activities can be very helpful to these pupils in enabling them to do this.

If you can give the pupil a position of responsibility in the group then this will also assist the development of mutual support and social responsibility and it will also foster a sense of trust.

Point out good role models

Do not assume that the pupil knows how to behave. You may need to teach him or her the behaviours which are required in school. If you can demonstrate yourself what is wanted or get him or her to copy another child who is behaving well then you will be demonstrating what is expected. Do not overdo this however – it can be very bad for self-esteem if it is always being pointed out that others do it right!

Try to anticipate trouble

Learn to recognise those situations in which problems for the pupil commonly arise, e.g. lining up at the door, coming in from break, being late for lessons. Help the pupil to recognise these situations for himself or herself and work out strategies for minimising or avoiding trouble. If a pupil can learn to keep out of the way of other pupils who seek confrontation, then this can make a tremendous difference to his or her life in school.

Deal with 'bad' behaviour in a positive way

By the very nature of their difficulties, children with behaviour problems will not always behave like the majority of the others and their anxiety or anger will 'spill over' in school. However, when incidents or confrontations do occur, it is important to deal with them in a calm and reasonable way. Remember to label the behaviour and not the child. Calling a child 'stupid', 'naughty', 'slow' or labelling them a 'bully' only serves to reinforce the idea in the child's mind that they are indeed those labels. The message must be 'I like you but I don't like your behaviour'. It is often helpful to talk about the effects the behaviour has had and the feelings it engenders in others: 'Jane, when you take money from the teacher's drawer it lets me down, and I'm sad about that because I want to trust you.'

Communicating your own feelings about the incident can be helpful: 'John, I feel angry when you mess about because you don't give me your best work and I know you can do better than this'.

Staying calm is *very* important. If you 'lose your cool' it will only serve to make the pupil feel worse and increase the likelihood of the incident occurring again.

Be realistic

Be realistic in setting goals for the pupil. Don't try to change all 'bad' behaviour at once. Choose one objective to start with (e.g. sitting in seat for five minutes, not shouting out for ten minutes). Be consistent; make it clear to the pupil what you are aiming for and reward the pupil if the target is achieved. Remember that it took a long time for the pupil to learn their patterns of behaviour, and overnight transformations are unlikely.

Helpful information and workshop activities for improving self-esteem in children can be found in a video workshop pack 'A Bag of Tricks' (Barbara Maines and George Robinson). There is a useful booklet to accompany the course: *You can – you know you can*, by Lucky Duck Publications. This may be accessible through the school's educational psychologist.

Supporting pupils with behaviour difficulties

You will need to work with the teacher in order to develop an Individual Behaviour Programme (IBP) or Pastoral Support Plan (PSP) for the pupil. You may be asked to do an observation of him or her in a particular lesson in order to find out exactly where the problems are coming from. The following framework provides a structure for deciding how to support the pupil. It works best if you can make this plan together with the class teacher and if you *both* carry it out.

Planning a structured behaviour programme for an individual pupil

There are a number of points to bear in mind when planning a behavioural programme.

The programme should be:

Workable	It should make sense to you and the pupil, and have clear targets. It will work best if all adults who work with the pupil are clear about the plan (teachers, parents, TAs).
Achievable	You should plan it so that the pupil is successful.
Realistic	Don't try to change all 'bad' behaviour at once. Start with one thing and work in steps towards success. It should be the right thing for the pupil in the situation, e.g. choosing 'staying in seat' when other pupils are moving round is not realistic.
Manageable	It should be easy for you to monitor and record results.

Step one – List

Write a short list of those behaviours you want to reduce. Next to these behaviours write the ones you want to see instead, e.g.:

Unwanted behaviours	Desired behaviours
Shouting out	Listening/working quietly
Getting out of seat	Staying in seat

Step two – Observe

Carry out an observation of the pupil. Become a 'fly on the wall' for half an hour and watch what is going on. Make a chart so that you can record what is happening. This will give you baseline information and provide a starting point. Below is an example of an observation chart:

Observation sheet

From this observation it would make sense to target shouting out as a priority. You may want to share these results with the pupil to agree you are aiming for a zero score but in the first week it might be more realistic to go for whatever reduction seems realistic and actionable. You would then explain to the pupil that the behaviour you want is 'keeping quiet in lesson time and raising hand to speak'.

Name: _____

Lesson: _____   Time of day: _____

	shouts out	out of seat	'on task'
10.00 – 10.05	3	2	3 mins
10.05 – 10.10	2	0	2 mins
10.10 – 10.15	2	1	1 min
10.15 – 10.20	0	0	0 mins
10.20 – 10.25	0	1	4 mins
10.25 – 10.30	2	2	2 mins
TOTAL	9	6	12/30

Step three – Review

Review your list in step one. You may have noticed other behaviours which will become priorities. Decide which particular behaviour you want to encourage, e.g. staying in seat, keeping hands to self, staying quiet and putting hand up to say something.

Step four – Environment analysis

Now look at what you might do to prevent this behaviour occurring in the first place. Consider whether you can change the location, peer group, subject or activity in order to eliminate or reduce the unwanted behaviour. For example:

- If a pupil always gets into trouble when seated next to another particular pupil then don't allow them to sit together.

- If a pupil starts distracting others shortly after a task has begun, ensure the task is clear and achievable when it is given.

- If a pupil finds it hard to get started on a task, ensure he/she has all equipment necessary before you start.

- Can any of the following be changed to prevent the behaviour happening in the first place?

Can these be changed?	YES	NO	HOW? and WHO?
Location of pupil (e.g. proximity to teacher)			
Location of pupil (sitting beside whom?)			
Subject lesson			
Task			
TA			
Teacher (e.g. parallel groups)			
Child's physical state			
Child's emotional state			

Step five – Teach new skills

Children need to be taught how to behave. You may need to demonstrate appropriate behaviour by role-play or by pointing out others modelling the right behaviour. The child may need considerable practice. An option to get this across could be role reversal, where you play the part of the child, and the child plays the adult. In this way they can improve his or her understanding of what is wanted. For example:

- 'This is how I want you to come into the classroom.' (demonstrate)

- 'I want you to keep your hands together on the table when I'm speaking, like this.' (demonstrate)

- 'I like the way John has started work straight away. I want you to do that.'

- 'I want you to keep quiet when I'm talking and put your hand up when you want to say something.'

Step six – Talk to the pupil

Share the results of your observation with the pupil. Explain that you are going to work together to encourage good behaviour, e.g. 'staying in seat' by cutting down the times he or she is out of his or her seat. Ask the pupil what needs to happen in order for them to stay in their seat. Involve the pupil in setting a target for the next similar lesson, i.e. cut down from eight to four the number of times the pupil gets out of their seat. Monitor and check how things are going – 'How's it going?' 'You're doing well.' 'You're remembering to sit in your seat. Well done.'

Other possibilities

Problem behaviour	Target behaviour (positively phrased)
Shouting out	Keep quiet and raise hand to speak
Out of seat	Stay in seat
Distracting others by poking	Keep hands, feet and objects to yourself
Seeking a great deal of adult attention	Work alone for five minutes

Step seven – Positive reinforcement of appropriate behaviour

Negotiate a reward for meeting the target (make the target easy to achieve). Ask the pupil what he or she would like as a reward. Suggest one if he or she doesn't come up with anything realistic. Suggestions for rewards are:

Infant/Junior

- bubble blowing;

- decorating plain biscuits with icing and sprinkles;

- extra time on the computer;

- a favourite game;
- music while you work;
- certificate to take home to parents;
- special responsibility.

Secondary

- extra computer time;
- pen;
- keyring;
- certificate to take home;
- cooking;
- special responsibility;
- free ticket to school disco.

The lottery principle

It is sometimes even more motivating if several rewards are possible, each written on a card and put in an envelope. One 'reward' should be extra special. The pupil takes a chance on choosing a reward and might get the 'star prize'.

Step eight – Praise

If the target is achieved give reward and praise and record on a chart for the pupil to see. Set a new target for next similar lesson, e.g. twice out of seat.

If the target is not achieved, make it easier and say 'We'll try again tomorrow'.

Step nine – Implementation

Continue for two weeks giving the negotiated reward for targets that are achieved. Review the programme. Continue to make targets clear and to teach any new behaviour skills the pupil needs and review environmental factors.

Step ten – Observe again

Do another observation and compare it with the original. Use the same lesson and same time of day. Is there any improvement? If not, why not? Consider appropriateness of task, peer group and environment.

Step eleven – Next steps

Choose another behaviour, e.g. 'Now that you're able to stay in your seat most of the time, we're going to choose another target. What do you think we could work on next?'

Remember to keep a written or picture record of what is achieved. The pupil might enjoy doing this themselves, e.g. putting stickers on a chart. Negotiate a 'super reward' for the pupil after two weeks of improvement. Send any good news home to share with parents as this is very effective.

Ensure the task the pupil is given is at the right level for his or her ability. Problems often occur when pupils are bored or the task is too hard.

Step twelve – Reactive strategy

If you have provided an optimum environment for the pupil, e.g. task at right level, sitting by non-troublemakers and the pupil still deliberately chooses not to follow an instruction then you will need to discuss with the teacher what sanction to apply. Reactive strategies are those which make the situation safe when everything else has failed, so it could be that removal from the situation, providing a calming environment or changing the task is necessary. So you might say: 'If you keep on getting up out of your seat, you will be moved away from the group.' Children and young people dislike being moved to sit away from their friends so this is quite an effective 'mild' sanction. This should only be done for short periods at a time. For more serious disruptive behaviour which has not responded to positive strategies, you may need to call the teacher or a school manager to support the removal of the pupil from the group for a period of calming. Following through with a sanction is very important. Evidence suggests that it is not the *severity* of the sanction but the *consistency* with which it is applied that makes the difference.

Attention Deficit Disorder

Attention Deficit Disorder (ADD), sometimes called Attention Deficit/Hyperactivity Disorder (AD/HD), is a label given to a certain set of behaviours, some of which are the same as those behaviours observed in children described as having social, emotional and behavioural difficulties. ADD is a term used to describe the condition of children and young people who have long-term difficulties in attention, hyperactivity and impulsive behaviour.

ADD is more 'behavioural' than 'emotional' and is thought to be caused by the biological make-up of the child, having its roots in neurology, whereas most social, emotional and mental health difficulties are thought to be a 'normal' reaction of the child to adverse external influences, although there are overlaps.

For ADD, three main factors are described:

- 'inattentive' means being easily distracted, not being able to concentrate or settle and being forgetful and disorganised;
- 'hyperactive' means being restless, fidgety and always 'on the go';
- 'impulsive' means having a tendency to interrupt, talk out of turn or be unable to wait.

ADD is a medical diagnosis. Difficulties should have been obvious for more than six months for a diagnosis to be made and should be apparent before the age of seven. Ritalin is often prescribed in order to help the pupil to concentrate and help him or her to settle to learn in school, although there can be side effects. As part of your work as a TA, one of your jobs might be to monitor the behaviour of the pupil who is taking Ritalin, and work with the teacher and the school nurse in doing this. Many adults who work with children are uncomfortable about controlling the behaviour of children using drugs and there is a view that too many children are identified as having ADD and sometimes it may seem like 'the medicalisation of social difficulties'.

It is important to manage these pupils in similar ways to other pupils with behavioural problems, and so all the advice given in the previous section is relevant. In fact it is important to plan 'behaviour modification programmes' and to judge their outcomes *before* drugs are prescribed, although this sometimes does not happen.

What are the learning implications?

- difficulty in concentrating;
- difficulty in following rules;
- talking out of turn or frequent calling out;
- losing or forgetting equipment;
- handing in work late, incomplete or sloppy;
- distracting others;
- getting out of seat.

How can I give support?

- Encouraging and giving frequent specific praise for effort and behaviour.
- Breaking tasks down into small chunks.
- Making instructions clear and simple.
- Sitting the pupil near the front under the teacher's view and next to a good role model.
- Using rewards to encourage good behaviour.
- Giving immediate sanctions for poor behaviour.
- Being calm and consistent.
- Thinking ahead about potentially difficult situations and how they might be managed.

Useful references for more detailed information about behaviour management are:

Attention Deficit/Hyperactivity Disorder:A Practical Guide for Teachers (1997) by Paul Cooper and Katherine Ideus, David Fulton Publishers.

Practical Strategies for Individual Behaviour Difficulties (1997) by Geraldine Mitchell, David Fulton Publishers.

Supporting Children with Behaviour Difficulties: A Guide for Assistants in Schools (2001) by Glenys Fox, David Fulton Publishers.

Supporting Children with Special Educational Needs (2003) by Marian Halliwell, David Fulton Publishers.

More information can be found at the National Attention Deficit Disorder Information and Support Service (ADDISS) www.addiss.org.uk.

For more information about mental health and well-being, see the Young Minds website: www.youngminds.org.uk.

Activity

- Choose a pupil you know who is causing concern.
- Plan a structured behavioural programme using the observation format and following the steps described in this chapter.
- Review progress after two weeks.
- Think of any pupils you work with who may have mental health problems. What signs have you spotted? Have you reported concerns to teachers?

CHAPTER 11

The role of school managers and special needs coordinators

Chapter summary

– What is good practice in managing teaching assistants?

– Mapping provision

– Use of intervention programmes

– Performance management

– What does research say about the best use of assistants?

– How can SENCOs and school managers make best use of teaching assistants?

– Provide regular opportunities for planning, discussion and evaluation with teacher colleagues

  – How can planning time be managed?

  – How can planning time be used effectively?

– Provide opportunities for training and development

– Useful resources

– Activity

'Schools wouldn't function without them!'

(SENCO junior school)

Head teachers, senior teachers and special needs coordinators (SENCOs) have a pivotal role to play in getting the best out of their teaching assistants (TAs). As we have noted earlier in this book, TAs are an expensive resource, so ensuring they are used effectively, efficiently and flexibly is a vital part of school development planning.

What is good practice in managing teaching assistants?

The advice to school managers in 2005 from the Primary Strategy entitled *The effective management of Teaching Assistants to improve standards in literacy and mathematics* is very helpful so I have included some of their good practice advice below.

(NB The Primary Strategy is no longer in use but the resources are available online.)

The following levers need to be in place to ensure schools and settings benefit fully from the contribution of teaching assistants.

- Effective leadership and management.
- Continuing professional development.
- Focused support for children and the use of evidence-based intervention programmes.
- Joint planning and reviewing progress.
- Monitoring impact.
- Performance management.

In schools where teaching assistants are used effectively there are clear management systems for ensuring:

- Induction and ongoing professional development opportunities.
- Identifying the needs of children across year groups and matching the deployment of teaching assistants and teachers to this analysis of need.
- Communication between teachers, teaching assistants, parents and the wider community.
- Monitoring and evaluating of the impact of teaching assistants.
- Inclusion of teaching assistants in performance management procedures.

Mapping provision

Mapping provision enables school managers to see the 'big picture' in terms of needs and resources, and to allocate resources (including teachers and TAs) through an evidence-based process. TA deployment will be related to the needs of particular cohorts of children – classes, groups and individuals. Provision mapping can be informed by the findings of audits of literacy and mathematics provision and the analysis of pupil performance data in literacy and numeracy. This will enable the effective targeting of TA support to raise standards in literacy and mathematics. Mapping in this way can show why it may be necessary to distribute teaching assistant support in ways other than, for example, one teaching assistant to one class. Effective targeting of intervention and support through provision mapping can lead to a significant reduction in the need for individual plans with a subsequent reduction in paperwork.

Use of intervention programmes

There is increasing evidence (e.g. from the EEF survey 2015) that focused, group intervention programmes delivered by trained teaching assistants have a significant impact on pupil achievement if the following factors are in place.

- The programme is selected based on evidence of its effectiveness and its match to children's needs.
- It has a time-limited focus.
- There is planned time for the teaching assistant to give feedback to the class teacher on progress and also to discuss any issues that have arisen.
- Its impact and use is regularly reassessed as part of provision mapping to identify whether teaching assistant time is justified in running particular programmes each year.
- It is part of whole school's provision to raise standards.

Some intervention programmes previously recommended by The National Strategies (now defunct but helpful resources still available) are time-limited, group intervention programmes which aim to accelerate progress up to age-related expectations, e.g. Catch Up Literacy. They are delivered by TAs working with small groups of carefully targeted children. Specific training in these programmes is a key feature of their effective use. Delivering these programmes enables teaching assistants to:

- develop their subject knowledge, pedagogical expertise and confidence;
- understand how the programme links to the ongoing work of the class;
- develop a shared understanding of the programme with the class teacher.

(The above is taken from the Primary Strategy 2005.)

Performance management

In most schools, the TA's time will be managed either by the Special Needs Coordinator (SENCO) or by a senior teacher. Day-to-day activities will usually be managed by the class teacher. The overall responsibility for how TAs are deployed lies with the head teacher. The SENCO will be guided by the Code of Practice 2015 (see Chapter 8). Over recent years, the role of the SENCO has become much more prescribed as a coordinator of learning support and as a manager of systems and resources. The latest Code of Practice reinforces this aspect of the job. For many SENCOs, a significant part of their role involves managing and advising a team of assistants, quality assuring their work and helping them to work in partnership with teaching staff.

There have been a number of studies on the impact of assistants. Some of the findings have significant implications for head teachers, SENCOs and teachers in the way assistance is used. School managers and SENCOs should review their use of assistants annually as they are 'worth their weight in gold', to quote one teacher … but only if they are used well. So how might SENCOs and school managers ensure that this is the case? Well, in effective schools, part of the performance management of TAs includes an observation of their work. By watching an assistant working with a pupil, or groups of pupils, the SENCO can see how effective they are in ensuring the pupil is learning as well as they can. They will be looking to see that the assistant has an encouraging manner, is sensitive to the pupil's needs and provides the right guidance for learning. This observation is part of a 'Quality Assurance' process. In recent years 'Quality Assurance' (QA) has become an important part of all aspects of school performance. School managers 'quality assure' the work of assistants through observation, making sure that their time is used to best effect.

What does research say about the best use of assistants?

The guidance report *Making Best Use of Teaching Assistants* (Education Endowment Foundation), published in 2015, and has significant implications for school managers and SENCOs. It has the following recommendations:

In the classroom

- TAs should not be used as an informal teaching resource for low attaining pupils.
- Use TAs to add value to what teachers do, not replace them.
- Use TAs to help pupils develop their independent learning skills and manage their own learning.
- Ensure TAs are fully prepared for their role in the classroom.

Delivering structured interventions out of class

- Use TAs to deliver high-quality, one-to-one and small-group support using structured interventions.
- Adopt evidence-based interventions to support TAs in their small group and one-to-one instruction.

Linking Learning

- Ensure explicit connections are made between learning from everyday classroom teaching and structured interventions.

Some of the practical implications for teachers are discussed in the next chapter.

When SENCOs are asked what is good practice in working with TAs; they identify the following factors as important.

SENCOs should ensure that assistants are:

- given regular opportunities for planning with teacher colleagues;
- clear about roles and responsibilities;
- valued as part of the learning team;
- clear about learning objectives;
- clear about the learning and emotional implications of the child's special need;
- considering the views of the pupil;
- deployed efficiently, effectively and flexibly;
- given opportunities for training and development.

Provide regular opportunities for planning, discussion and evaluation with teacher colleagues

This is such an important issue. All the many reports published since the 1980s make the key point that the sharing of lesson planning is vital and that, where extra adult help is provided, planning and communication are the keys to improving its impact.

We don't really need to be telling this – it is sound common sense and yet it still does not happen enough in our schools. It is an issue raised frequently and has been referred to a number of times in previous chapters. The role of the school manager or SENCO is to ensure that there is *time* for planning and *time* to ensure that lesson plans and individual learning or behaviour plans are communicated to those TAs who will implement the plans and, as a result, become real and effective. SENCOs need to negotiate this with the other members of staff and help them to understand the importance of such planning. Discussions with both teachers and TAs highlight the importance of time spent together in order to plan, monitor and evaluate individual learning programmes and the role of the TA in lessons. These meetings should be on at least a weekly basis and, in some cases, on a daily basis. If, as SENCO, you feel that not enough or even no time is allocated for this purpose, then it is clearly an issue that should be addressed with the head teacher and with the other members of staff in your school.

The 2005 report on the Primary National Strategies identified many different ways and contexts in which joint planning and reviewing can be undertaken. These are also relevant for secondary managers and include:

- termly or half-termly reviews;
- involvement in in-service training days;
- timetabled weekly meetings;
- ongoing informal feedback during and after sessions;

How can SENCOs and school managers make best use of teaching assistants?

How can planning time be managed?

- a shared booklet or recorded memos;
- computer-based records.

Joint planning and reviewing progress between teachers and teaching assistants, both at whole-school and class level, helps to ensure:

- a consistent approach;
- opportunities for each adult to share their particular knowledge and expertise;
- any group or individual work is integrated into whole-class work, where appropriate and relevant links are made;
- focused differentiation and support is identified;
- assessment opportunities and techniques are identified and detailed assessment information is built up;
- curricular targets and success criteria are jointly understood;
- learning and teaching can be adjusted in the light of feedback.

How can planning time be used effectively?

The lesson plans and individual plans for pupils form a sound base for discussion. SENCO or school managers need to give some thought to whether it is better to meet with individual TAs or teachers to discuss pupil issues or whether small groups can gain from each other's experience – there is probably a place for both ways of working, depending on pupil needs. There is one particular principle to be recommended when reviewing the arrangements for each child and evaluating effectiveness: 'If it works, do more of it. If it doesn't work, do something different.' Set clear, achievable objectives involving the pupil and the TA in this process if possible. This forms the basis of a useful plan. The next step is to consider how best to put the plan into practice.

Clear about roles and responsibilities

An important part of the role as a school manager or SENCO is to provide a clear *job description* (see Appendix A) which describes the TA's duties in four areas:

- supporting the pupil;
- supporting the teacher;
- supporting the curriculum;
- supporting the school.

This can be extremely useful in setting the framework within which the TA will work. Fundamental to this is an understanding of the *purpose* of assistance, which is to promote effective learning for all and assist and support inclusion of pupils with disadvantaged or special educational needs. It will be important at the outset to make clear to assistants the degree of sensitivity which the role requires – the job is not to be a minder or a personal servant for pupils but to encourage independence and self-reliance. Certainly it needs to be made clear that the TA is not there to do the work for the pupil and that sometimes allowing the pupil to get things wrong might be a valuable part of the learning experience.

In doing their job, assistants will value your advice on the practical aspects of working as an extra adult in the classroom in order to avoid feeling uncomfortable or, worse still, unwanted. Certain ground rules will need to be established with the class teacher (subject teachers, if in secondary) and the SENCO can arrange for this to be negotiated at the start of the school year so that the assistant does not feel 'thrown in at the deep end' (see Chapter 1 for 'Ground rules').

School managers need to ensure that effective and appropriate induction training is provided for new TAs and that experienced TAs get ongoing professional development opportunities (see Chapter 13). SENCOs need to ensure that the assistants understand routines and procedures which operate within the school – from safeguarding to fire drills – and more local systems, such as reading schemes and library use.

Another consideration is that of responsibility for the individual plan; TAs should be made aware that it is not their responsibility to devise, develop, monitor or evaluate the learning programmes for the pupil, but that their main role will be to support the implementation of the programme. It is good practice for the assistants to be involved at all these stages and to be confident enough to add their observations and ideas to any plans. The professional responsibility, however, lies with the class teacher and SENCO.

Valued as part of the team

Any management textbook will tell you that good management involves motivating your staff. Motivation develops as a direct result of feeling valued and confident in the job – having the skills and knowing the routines. Assistants feel valued when they are included as part of school teams and accepted as part of the school staff. SENCOs can do a lot to make assistants feel confident and creative by providing opportunities for sharing planning processes and asking for their views. TA attendance at annual reviews and case conferences has been very helpful when the contribution has been planned with the SENCO beforehand. This sort of involvement leads to a more committed and motivated staff.

Many SENCOs and school managers have developed annual performance reviews for assistants, as described above. This provides an opportunity for celebrating success as well as giving improvement suggestions and constructive criticism. As a two-way process, it will also give assistants the chance to share their views about how to improve arrangements and to feel valued.

Clear about the learning objectives

Consider this analogy – if you were setting out on a journey you would plan a route and a destination. If you didn't know where you were going or how to get there you would become confused, frustrated and angry and the journey would take much longer. Just as for a journey, you need a destination and a route, so for a child to learn effectively the adult delivering the learning programme must know the 'destination', i.e. the learning objectives and the best route. This will mean developing an awareness of the learning style of the pupil – whether they learn best through visual, auditory or tactile cues, or a combination. And just as the time of day the journey is taken might affect the route and the time it takes, so for a learning programme the supporting adult should be sensitive to the best time of day for effective intervention. This is particularly important with younger children, e.g. a TA implementing a speech and language programme will probably find the child more receptive to a short session early on in the school day.

Clear about the learning and emotional implications of the child's special need

Each type of special need has associated implications for learning and it is important that the TA is made aware of these implications so that realistic learning objectives can be set, e.g. a pupil who has specific learning difficulties is likely to have great difficulty in copying from the board; a pupil with cerebral palsy is likely to have perceptual difficulties. The SENCO has an important role in providing the TA with information about different special needs and which approaches work best. This can be supported by helpful handouts and discussion. TAs value regular meetings led by the SENCO where they can share any concerns with each other and get advice about working with pupils.

All children want to belong to the wider group. SENCOs need to help assistants recognise when a child is settled and happy and to understand that emotional factors can override the learning plan. TAs should be encouraged to work in such a way as to downplay any differences and encourage inclusion as much as possible. Judging how the child works best, whether in class or out of class in small groups, is an important task. The child must feel settled before learning can take place.

Consider the views of the pupil

In discussing how best to manage assistance, it is also of vital importance to consider the views of the pupil, so SENCOs need to involve pupils when planning any programme. This is especially true for older pupils who can clearly say what they would prefer. For younger children, the TA may be able to speak on behalf of the child. In secondary schools, students seem to hold one of two views. Firstly, there are those who like nothing better than to have additional support in subjects they find hard and are quite happy for this to be given in a class setting, often preferring that the TA is seen working with others at times or with small groups. Secondly, there are other students who absolutely hate being singled out as different in any way from the rest of the group. Conformity and belonging to the group is so important for most adolescents that anything which can lead to derision by others is rejected. This issue spans a number of areas (dress, hairstyle, eating habits, etc. – ask any parent!) Be aware of these issues which relate to belonging and self-esteem and endeavour to use assistance sensitively. Sometimes working outside the main group (out of sight, out of mind) enables the young person to relax and this provides a better learning context.

Checklist for action – managing TAs in the classroom

Action by SENCOs	Action by schools	Already in place?	Action required?
SENCO and TA have agreed on the lessons in which there is a role for the TA.			
Role of the TA has been planned.			
Teacher or TA prepare special materials if necessary.			
	Time is allocated for planning and communication between teacher and TA.		
	School manager/SENCO observe impact of TAs in classroom on pupils. Also out of classroom delivering specific programmes.		

(Based on: Audit Commission/HMI, 1992b.)

Deployed efficiently, effectively and flexibly

Things can go wrong if assistance is badly managed. Plans may be perfect but unless they are put into practice they remain just pieces of paper. So how can SENCOs and school managers ensure that assistance is deployed efficiently, effectively and flexibly to actively support learning?

In some cases, there can be more than one additional adult in the classroom, and this presents the teacher with a more complex management task. Support from the SENCO is needed in discussing the 'how to' in this case. What is necessary here is a well-planned but flexible negotiation of adult roles, and advance planning is crucial. In one observed Year 7 group of twenty students, there were four adults in the classroom – one teacher, one support teacher for a child with hearing impairment and two assistants to support students with behavioural difficulties. This was not an efficient, effective or flexible lesson, mainly because the teacher did not assume authority over the group and the students did not seem to know where the authority was vested. There had obviously been no planning. With some forward planning, this lesson would have been much better. For any lesson with more than just the class teacher, the adults need to agree beforehand:

- What are the learning objectives for this lesson?
- Who will assume overall authority, introduce the lesson and delegate the tasks?
- Who will work with whom?
- Who will be responsible for resources?
- What particular strengths will each bring to benefit individuals/the group and at what time in the lesson this will be appropriate?
- When will the assistant(s) intervene and when will they observe?
- How to use differentiated material depending on the range of abilities in the group.
- What to do if a pupil becomes disruptive.

If, as a school manager or SENCO, you can steer the effective and efficient deployment of TAs it will certainly lead to improved progress, a wider range of activities for pupils, better differentiation according to ability, and teamwork in the classroom.

Provide opportunities for training and development

(See also Chapter 13.) One of the most consistent messages coming from TAs who have had no training is that they lack confidence in what they do. This can be inhibiting and prevents participation and creativity. It is a particular problem for assistants who are newly appointed and unsure of their role. The need for providing encouragement and training is clear if confidence is to be boosted.

As a school manager or SENCO, you might consider formalising a system of teachers as mentors, especially for newly appointed assistants.

If used to best effect, the resources of your TAs can make a significant difference to the school experience of disadvantaged pupils and those with SEN. If, as a school manager or SENCO, you take time to ensure TAs are clear about their job – what to do, when to do it and how to work – and to provide training to develop their skills, these investments will result in a more effective learning experience for the pupils and a motivated and committed team of assistants.

Useful resources

The Training and Development Agency (TDA) produced a helpful resource kit for school managers to use. (Effective Deployment of School

Staff. TDA 2010. NB The TDA no longer exists but the resources can still be found online.)

The kit includes:

How effective is our classroom practice?
This section looks at the clarity of roles and responsibilities in the classroom and the extent to which the classroom team jointly plans and prepares.

How effectively do we develop our existing workforce?
This section looks at the extent to which continuing professional development (CPD) is used to develop effective classroom support and how well performance review processes encourage and support effective deployment.

How well do we plan and recruit?
This section looks at the extent to which a school plans the roles required within it and how the workforce is deployed, together with the extent to which recruitment processes match identified need.

Maximising the Impact of Teaching Assistants (MITA)
This website (www.maximisingtas.co.uk) contains auditing tools to help schools, details of courses and conferences, a blog and downloadable papers and articles for practitioners on the extensive research at the UCL Institute of Education, London.

Help in the Classroom
Margaret Balshaw, in her book *Help in the Classroom* (1991), has some activities and scenarios which encourage schools to look at principles of good practice in order to encourage partnership working and to plan more efficient and effective ways of using assistance.

Activity

- Use the checklist for action in this chapter to review the use of TAs in your school.
- Read the report on maximising the impact of TAs and assess whether your TAs are being used to best effect.

The role of the teacher working with the teaching assistant

Chapter summary

- What do teachers say about working with TAs?
- What do teachers want TAs to do more of?
- What advice would teachers give to new TAs?
- What can teachers learn from research about TAs?
- How can the teacher best support the TA?
  - Ensuring that the TA is clear about his or her responsibilities in the classroom
  - Providing regular opportunities for planning and discussion
  - Encouraging the work of the TA and providing positive feedback
  - Making sure the TA knows the learning support implications of any pupil's special need
  - Making clear and realistic requests
  - Being part of a team
  - Some pitfalls
- Activity

It is clear that teaching assistants (TAs) have become a valuable and enduring part of school life. The great majority of teachers appreciate the support they get from TAs and cannot imagine school life without them.

'I really value the TAs I work with. They give me and the children amazing support. I couldn't teach half as well without them.'

(junior school TA)

Looking back, it seems strange to think that TAs have only been around in mainstream schools since the early 1980s, following the 1981 Education Act and the impetus that act gave to supporting more children with special educational needs in these schools. A range of reports since then, e.g. from HMI, university researchers and the Primary National Strategy, show that well-trained and well-managed teaching assistants can have a significant impact on inclusion, children's achievements and attitudes, and teacher workload.

As we noted in Chapter 4: 'Supporting the teacher', TAs work with teachers to:

- foster the participation of all pupils in the social and academic practices of the school or setting;
- help raise the standards and achievement of all pupils;
- encourage independent learning.

However, there is a big issue here. The effectiveness of TAs depends significantly on how they are deployed by the class teacher. So it is vital for teachers to plan proactively how assistants can best be used. Where the teacher's management is not effective, this potential to make a difference is not fully realised and an expensive resource is wasted.

In most secondary schools, the special needs coordinator (SENCO) has the responsibility for managing the overall workload of the TAs, and most TA time is spent in class working under the direction of subject teachers. In primary schools and early years settings it is mainly class teachers who guide TA activities, often with SENCO input. So it is very important that teachers consider how best they can work with their assistants. It is the teacher's job to direct pupil's work in all lessons and to negotiate the role of the TA in delivering the curriculum to the class. This negotiation about what part the assistant will play depends on two things: the needs of the pupils and the support needed by the teacher to deliver the lesson.

What do teachers say about working with TAs?

Teachers in secondary schools report that they have support from assistants in over half of all lessons. All say that the support helps students to learn with over half reporting that it helps a lot. Most TA time in secondary school lessons is a combination of general support, support for pupils who have special educational needs and those who have pupil premium funding. Some assistants deliver specific programmes, e.g. 'Accelerated Reader'. Three quarters of secondary teachers had no specific training in how to make best use of assistance, although the same proportion would welcome such training. Nearly all secondary school teachers said that there is not enough time to plan together with assistants.

Teachers in primary schools and early years settings have support from assistants in nearly all lessons. All say that TAs help a lot, many say they are indispensable. As for secondary schools, the role involves a combination of support roles. However, more primary assistants run small-group or individual intervention programmes. About half of primary teachers had no specific training in how to make best use of assistance although some younger teachers had training as part of their teacher training courses. Fewer than half would like training in how best to use assistance as they think working relationships are effective. Nearly all primary school teachers said that they make time to discuss lessons with the TAs although much of this is in conversation rather than written down. Lesson plans and learning objectives are shared more in primary schools.

What do teachers want TAs to do more of?

When asked what teachers would like assistants to do more of, several gave responses such as '*stepping back to encourage independence*', and to do less of '*stepping in with the answers*.' In lessons, the main thing that teachers want is for assistants to be proactive rather than reactive. Secondly, they want them to understand how children learn. Good literacy and numeracy skills are also desirable. Teachers also want assistants to address low-level disruptive behaviour, using the same approach as them.

> '*I need my assistant to respond to pupil need, be consistent in expectations of behaviour, to have authority and react calmly.*'
>
> *(secondary teacher)*

What advice would teachers give to new TAs?

The main piece of advice that teachers would give to someone starting out as a TA would be to research the learning needs of the pupil. Another key piece of advice is to ask when they are not sure. Half report that joint planning is a key aspect of partnership working and a third think that clarity of roles is important. Although it is becoming more widespread, over half do not give lesson plans or schemes of work to assistants.

> '*Get literacy and numeracy skilled and a wide variety of experience.*'
>
> *(primary teacher)*

What can teachers learn from research about TAs?

The Education Endowment Foundation guidance report 'Making Best use of Teaching Assistants' (2015) provides a range of evidence of how TAs can have the most impact on learning. There are implications for school managers and SENCOs in respect of whole school policy on managing TAs (see Chapter 11) but there are some findings which teachers can implement. The report has more detail but the key points for teachers to take account of are as follows:

> '*TAs tend to be more concerned with task completion and less concerned with developing understanding.*'

In observing TAs at work, the researchers noted that some TAs tend to close down talk and 'spoon-feed' answers. Teachers report that this is often the case so they need to step in and help the TA to be less concerned with task completion and more concerned with developing pupils' understanding and thinking skills. Encouraging and modelling the use of effective questions to guide learning is also key to TA effectiveness. As some pupils learn at a slower pace than others it can be very tempting for the TA to do the work for them, but this needs to be discouraged by the teacher.

> '*TA support may increase dependency.*'

It is very important for the teacher to spot when a pupil is becoming too dependent on an assistant. This may be resolved by changing the TA or having a word with the TA to help him or her realise that it is not helping the pupil in terms of responsibility for learning and separation from classmates. A degree of sensitivity is required here. There are times when one-to-one is helpful but it is important that it is not overused. As noted in Chapter 2, pupils can quickly get used to someone else doing the work.

'Use TAs to deliver high-quality, one-to-one and small-group support using structured interventions.'

One key recommendation of the report highlights the point that TAs can be very effective in promoting learning if they are trained to deliver small-group structured interventions. Examples come from 'Catch-up' programmes for literacy and numeracy. TAs report that they enjoy leading these activities as they can see the benefits to pupils. Teachers should recognise the value of this support and work with the SENCO to set up such interventions.

'Ensure explicit connections are made between learning from everyday classroom teaching and structured interventions.'

This follows from the previous point. Any learning outside the classroom needs to be consolidated by linking it to in-lesson work as appropriate. This reinforces the learning for the pupil.

'Use TAs to add value to what teachers do, not replace them.'

In some lessons, where group work is part of the activity, it is not unusual for the TA to be assigned to work with the least able pupils. The teacher needs to consider whether this is the best use of teacher time. It is often more useful for the teacher to work with the least able pupils, allowing the TA to circulate the rest of the class, keeping pupils on task. Flexibility is the key, as is recognition by the teacher that all pupils require teacher attention in the lesson, particularly those who find it hardest to learn.

Teaching assistants report that the most effective teachers are the ones who:

How can the teacher best support the TA?

- Share planning;
- Give clear directions;
- Value contributions;
- Welcome feedback;
- Encourage questions;
- Use TA strengths.

Teachers who work with TAs identify the following aspects of their role:

- ensuring the TA is clear about his or her responsibilities in the classroom;
- providing regular opportunities for planning and discussion;
- encouraging the work of the TA and providing positive feedback;
- making sure the TA knows any learning support implications of the pupil's special need;

- making clear and realistic requests;
- valuing the TA as part of a team.

Ensuring that the TA is clear about his or her responsibilities in the classroom

When teachers start their first teaching appointment, it is after considerable time has been spent in training and teaching practice. However, some assistants have not had any training when they start work and their experience of school life may well be limited to their own school days. So, a TA who is new to the job will need a period of induction where 'on the job' training will be required. The TA may not understand the frameworks within which schools operate and will need help in understanding a wide range of issues from, for instance, the process and content of the national curriculum or how to share a book with a child. In practical subjects the assistant will need to be shown how to use equipment correctly and to understand safety procedures.

It is very important and helpful to both the teacher and the TA if the ground rules for working together are negotiated at the start of each school year (see Chapter 1, 'What Are the Ground Rules?'). This is more of a task in secondary schools where assistants have more teachers to work with. Some secondary schools now allocate assistants to departments so there is more familiarity with both the staff and the curriculum. This is not always possible when assistance is linked to individual pupils although some schools now split responsibilities when an individual pupil has a high level of support. This means that the pupil does not become too dependent on just one adult.

Providing regular opportunities for planning and discussion

The importance of regular meetings for planning, monitoring and evaluating the work of the TA is vital and is the key to ensuring a high-quality learning experience for all pupils who need learning support. Ideally, the teacher, the assistant and the SENCO will have meetings every so often in order to do this – this is often built into reviewing pupil plans. On a daily or weekly basis, however, the teacher and assistant need to negotiate who does what in the lesson (see Chapter 11 for more on joint planning). The teacher will certainly need to consider how best to use the assistant. This could be in working with an individual child, or with a small group. Or again it could be preparing appropriate worksheets or resources for the pupils who need additional support. As discussed earlier, research tells us that TAs are most effective when they deliver specific programmes with prescribed teaching notes, but they also need very clear directions by the teacher. As we have noted, there is usually little time for joint planning but it can prove very helpful if, as a teacher, you can:

- Write the TA role into the lesson plan and give a copy to the TA.
- Write brief notes on post-its and give them to the TA at the start of the lesson.

- Have an informal chat just before the lesson, or maybe when the pupils are arriving and settling in.

- Give the scheme of work to the TA to read so that they know what to expect in advance.

- Encourage the TA to ask for guidance when they are not sure what to do.

- Take time to meet with the TA occasionally, to share notes on the pupils who are being supported and to listen to the TA's ideas on how that support could be enhanced.

Encouraging the work of the TA and providing positive feedback

Most TAs, particularly when new to the role, admit to feeling under-confident about their work. This is usually because they have been away from the workplace for some time and also because they have had no training about what to expect, either in terms of the role they will fulfil or about the special needs they will meet. Encouragement from teachers is important in order to build confidence. Positive feedback about what has worked well and constructive criticism provided as 'improvement suggestions' can work wonders in transforming unsure assistants into enthusiastic and confident colleagues.

Making sure the TA knows the learning support implications of any pupil's special need

Each type of need has associated implications for learning support. It is important that the teacher explains these implications to the TA so that realistic outcomes can be expected from the learning tasks. For instance, a pupil with emotional problems may achieve very little academically on some days. On such occasions a 'listening ear' may do much more in supporting the pupil than insistence on the completion of a task.

Knowing the learning implications entails providing work for the pupil at the right level so that success is likely. The TA may have good ideas about how best to modify the task or worksheet to make it more accessible for some pupils. It is important that the teacher makes clear to the TA just what the purpose of the learning task is so that alternatives can be considered if necessary. TAs often have ideas which can add value to lessons.

Making clear and realistic requests

When asked about issues which prevent effective partnerships from working, TAs report that they are sometimes asked to do tasks which they feel they cannot do, either because they are unclear about the task or because they feel they do not have the expertise. As a teacher, therefore, do not assume that the TA has psychic powers but make requests clear, checking that the TA has understood. Encourage the TA to ask if they are not sure. Remember that it is the responsibility of the teacher to decide the teaching methods, the materials to be used and the recording system. It is also the responsibility of the teacher to manage and monitor the work of the TA in the classroom. This can only be done effectively if communication is clear and realistic and if the TA is not overburdened with responsibilities which clearly belong with the teacher.

Being part of a team

It is important that the TA is encouraged to see himself or herself as part of a team in supporting both the lesson and any pupils with particular needs. The class teacher can encourage this perception by valuing the views of the TA and ensuring that the perspective of the TA is shared whenever there is a full case discussion about the pupil. This may be as part of an individual learning or behaviour programme, an Annual Review or a case conference. The class teacher has a role in encouraging other members of staff and also the parents to have a positive view of the TA as a colleague who works in partnership with teachers and parents to meet children's needs.

Some pitfalls

Margaret Balshaw in her book *Help in the Classroom* (1991) describes several scenarios where things go wrong for the assistant as a result of the teacher's mis-management of the situation. Four such scenarios are as follows:

The overgrown pupil

This is when the assistant is ignored in terms of his or her support role and treated almost as though he or she were another child in the group. As a teacher, you should be aware of the role the assistant can play and assistants must beware of acting like an 'overgrown' pupil.

Piggy in the middle

This is when the assistant feels like the 'go-between'. This occurs when the teacher assumes that the responsibility for the pupil lies solely with the assistant. The assistant finds himself or herself overburdened and unsupported. It also happens when the teacher gives an activity for the assistant to carry out with the child or group of children and, not long into the activity, the TA realises that the task is not 'matched' to the pupils and feels awkward in having to report back. These difficulties can be avoided by joint planning and good communication. The SENCO has a part to play here in making clear the respective responsibilities of the teacher and the assistant and facilitating planning time.

Spy in the classroom

This is a rare occurrence these days as teachers are used to having TAs in their lessons. This 'spy in the classroom' situation occurs when the teacher may feel that the assistant is in some way 'spying' on him or her and there is a resulting mistrust between the adults involved. It is important that the adults work together to support the children and that any personal difficulties can be ironed out. This can be done by involving a third party, e.g. the SENCO.

Dogsbody

This is when the TA is used by the teacher in a way which is perceived as unfair. There are occasions, still described, when teachers have used assistants to escort disruptive pupils from the classroom and 'mind' them for some time. This may very occasionally be appropriate if this has been negotiated beforehand or if the TA is employed to work with a particular pupil who is disruptive, but it is a problem raised by a number of TAs. Using an assistant as a classroom 'skivvy' is also unacceptable. They will generally be very pleased to help clear up but clearing up should be recognised as the responsibility of pupils and teachers too.

It must be said that these scenarios are the exception rather than the rule, although it is clear from work done with TAs that their view of their roles and responsibilities is not always the same as that of the teacher.

The following activities will be useful in establishing common ground. It is for both teachers and TAs to complete separately, then to compare notes to identify any mismatch. It then can guide discussion about how best to support each other.

ACTIVITY 1

You are a teacher/an assistant (ring as appropriate).
Please read the following statements and give a rating to each statement:

The TA you work with is: OR as a TA I am:	not at all	not much	just OK	pretty much
• clear about roles and responsibilities;	1	2	3	4
• valued as part of the learning support team;	1	2	3	4
• given regular opportunities for planning with teacher colleagues;	1	2	3	4
• clear about learning objectives;	1	2	3	4
• deployed efficiently, effectively, flexibly;	1	2	3	4
• given opportunities for training and development.	1	2	3	4

Now compare your ratings with the teacher/TA you work with and discuss which areas can be improved for you both and how you might work better together.

ACTIVITY 2

As a teacher, do you:

- share planning;
- give clear directions;
- value contributions;
- welcome feedback;
- encourage questions;
- use TA strengths?

CHAPTER 13

The professional development needs of teaching assistants

Chapter summary

- The need for support
- The need for encouragement
- Performance management
- The need for training and development
- Training
    - What background experience do I need?
    - What training do I need?
    - What training would TAs like?
    - When should training take place?
    - What training is available?
    - How can schools help?
    - Mentors
    - What should training include?
    - Who can best deliver this training?
- Higher level teaching assistants
- Useful links
- Activity

You may be so busy fulfilling your support role with the pupil, the teacher, the curriculum and the school that you may overlook the fact that you yourself have professional development needs – needs which include support, encouragement and training.

The need for support

The teacher or SENCO with whom you work has a big influence on whether you feel well-supported or not. Those parts of your work affected by this relationship are addressed in earlier chapters. Essentially, you need support to know what you have to do, how you need to do it and how successful you have been. It is sometimes quite easy to find out the 'what' and 'how' of a task but it is often quite difficult to know whether you have done a good job or not. Accept advice, know your limitations and those of the pupil, use your initiative to seek alternatives and ask for feedback on what you have done.

You will feel well-supported if your school does the following:

- *Provides you with a clear job description* (see Appendix A).

- *Uses your time well:*

  i.e. not 9–10 a.m. then 2–3 p.m. on the same day. This means that your time is not wasted sitting through whole school events when you could be preparing materials.

- *Provides a permanent contract:*

  Many teaching assistants (TAs) are employed on temporary contracts and this is unsatisfactory. There will always be children in our schools who need additional learning support. However, temporary contracts are sometimes the result of the uncertainty head teachers have about school funding, which varies from year to year.

- *Provides adequate conditions of service:*

  Even in these enlightened days there are still a minority of TAs who feel exploited, e.g. by having to do daily playground duties in their own break-times. If you feel you are being unfairly treated, discuss it with other TAs who may feel the same, then discuss it with the SENCO or another senior teacher.

- *Provides career development opportunities:*

  Many schools include TAs in relevant in-service training events and most TAs value these opportunities. Through training, you might feel encouraged to do more courses and gain experience in working with different sorts of needs – you might decide to go for additional qualifications. Some TAs have been inspired to train as teachers.

- *Acts quickly to prevent confusion:*

  When problems or misunderstandings arise, it is important that the issues are dealt with speedily and with fairness. In discussion with groups of assistants, it is clear that a number are confused about aspects of their work in schools. Much depends, of course, on the ability of the class teacher to know how best to use assistance. There will be some systems and personalities in schools which are resistant to change, but there will always be *some* changes you can effect. In endeavouring to do this, you will need all those qualities described earlier in this book. (See Chapter 2, 'What makes an effective TA?') Constructive criticism, couched in the form of 'improvement suggestions', will often be welcomed.

The following causes of confusion are frequently raised. Some possible solutions are offered:

CAUSES OF CONFUSION	HOW TO PREVENT CONFUSION
1 Lack of background information.	**1** Ask questions. Look at school records. Look at individual plans.
2 No 'named' person to relate to or too many people telling you what to do.	**2** Negotiate support from a nominated teacher.
3 Breakdown in communication.	**3** Agree arbitrator to resolve difficulties/conflicts.
4 Lack of joint planning.	**4** Request time for joint planning.
5 Lack of trust.	**5** Encourage trust through consistent supportive work and readiness to work collaboratively.
6 Lack of support.	**6** Form a support group with TAs in your school or in neighbouring schools. Make your 'special needs' known to the SENCO or a senior teacher.
7 Unclear expectations of staff.	**7** Planning, clear job description, clear timetable. Make staff aware of how you are able to work – the SENCO can help you with this. Know your limitations. Use your strengths.
8 Unclear *how* to work with pupil.	**8** Ask the teacher to demonstrate.
9 Unhelpful labelling, e.g. 'Mark's special helper'.	**9** Negotiate your 'label' (see 'Chapter 1', Ground Rules).
10 Assumptions made that the TA has specialist knowledge.	**10** Admit when you don't know; seek information from teachers and TAs.
11 No 'targets' set for the pupil.	**11** Find out, by asking, what realistic expectations are and what objectives or targets should be set.
12 No training.	**12** Ask to attend relevant in-service training in and out of school. Read books. Visit other schools to share good practice.

The need for encouragement

From discussion with TAs, it is clear that the job can be fulfilling, creative and rewarding. On the other hand it can be confusing, frustrating and demoralising. Most assistants seem to find themselves somewhere between these two extremes. When asked, the majority of teachers say how much they value the support and skills which TAs offer, but there is one problem – often enough, they don't tell the TAs that. Too few schools provide constructive feedback on a regular basis to their TAs. This lack of encouragement from school staff is not deliberate but often happens. This is because, on the one hand, time is not routinely allocated for evaluation of TA input and also because teachers themselves do not receive enough positive feedback. (You can support the teacher by providing some of this!)

One of the most consistent messages coming from TAs who have had no training is that they lack confidence in what they do. This can be very inhibiting and prevents participation and creativity. It is a particular problem for TAs who are newly appointed and who are unsure of their role. The need for creating regular opportunities to review progress and provide encouragement is clear if confidence is to be boosted.

'Simply the best'

Performance management

Teachers undergo an annual process of appraisal called Performance Management. They have meetings, usually twice a year, with their line manager to discuss their effectiveness and their teaching is observed by a senior manager in the school to assess how well they are teaching and how well the pupils are learning. This process has been extended in the majority of schools to review the work of TAs, allowing time for celebration of success, setting targets and encouraging future projects. It is also a forum for identifying professional development needs and relevant courses or experience.

The need for training and development

'Gone are the days when you could just employ a 'nice mum', it's not enough, you need to know more about how schools work and how children learn.'

(junior school TA)

Evidence from a range of surveys shows that teaching assistants are more likely to have the skills and knowledge to support pupil learning effectively if they have received appropriate induction training and continuing professional development. It is now universally acknowledged that TAs need to be trained in the form of induction training when they start their jobs and then access to continuing professional development (CPD) according to their roles and responsibilities. In good schools, training time is included in TAs' contracted hours.

The Primary Strategy report on the management of teaching assistants (2004) has these helpful guidelines about training:

Training for teaching assistants should:

- be planned, systematic and cumulative;
- be identified in the school development plan and individual performance management portfolios;
- relate to identified national, school and personal priorities;
- over time, contain a balance of general and subject-specific training, including developing subject knowledge;
- be monitored for impact and effectiveness;
- include opportunities for teachers and TAs to undertake joint professional development within and beyond the school. It is important that teaching assistants should have good subject knowledge to enable them to support pupils' learning. This includes secure standards of literacy and numeracy.

(See the Primary National Strategy report, 'The effective management of Teaching Assistants to improve standards in literacy and mathematics in Year 6' [DfES 0340-2004].)

Training

TAs vary greatly in their background experience. A number are trained teachers who do not want the responsibility of a full class and full-time working. Some have no formal qualifications at all. Research by the National Foundation for Educational Research (NFER,

What background experience do I need?

Fletcher–Campbell) has shown that assistants range from ex-dinner ladies or parent volunteers who want more involvement with classroom life to people considering a career in teaching and who are exploring this by way of working as an assistant. Others are qualified teachers who wish to return to teaching following a career break and who see an assistant's role as a way of getting back into schools. Nearly all TAs have experience of working with children either in school, e.g. as parent helpers, as 'dinner ladies', or through voluntary agencies, e.g. Brownies, and the majority bring very important parenting skills to their role. This wide variation in background experience shows a clear need for training, especially since the role has become more educational, with assistants being much more involved in the child's learning. The following scenario highlights this need:

> *An assistant described a discussion between the class teacher, the parents of a child with special needs and herself. She was asked by the parents what particular training she had had in order for her to support their child and she had to say that she had no special training and had to rely on the guidance of the class teacher.*

Parents need to know that their children are supported by people who know what they are doing. Schools need to be sure that children who need assistance are given informed and confident support from fully trained assistants.

Whatever their background experience, there are still some assistants who start the job with no specific training either about the role or about the range of needs they might meet. Most assistants are now given some sort of induction once they have started the job, but also learn by 'trial and error' on a day-to-day basis and by watching teachers at work.

What training do I need?

All TAs need continuing professional development. It is up to schools and local authorities to decide what qualifications and experience applicants for TA jobs need and a lot depends on the particular role. Some schools employ TAs on the basis of their past experience, sometimes because they started as a 'helping mum' and have proved to have good communication skills with children. Other schools may require a qualification as part of the job specification. You can use the activity at the end of this chapter to clarify your own training needs.

What training would TAs like?

New TAs value good induction programmes. Experienced TAs report that they would value more specific training, e.g. in maths or English curriculum areas or in working with pupils who have social, emotional or behavioural needs. A number of TAs would like more information and training on special educational needs, notably mental health needs, autism and Asperger's syndrome as there are now more pupils in mainstream schools with these needs.

In an ideal world TAs would be trained before taking up an appointment or as soon as possible once appointed. In-school 'informal' training, of course, starts on day one, but 'formal' training should be provided for all assistants as soon as it can be arranged.

In responding to the UNISON survey (2013), 75 per cent of TAs expressed concern over lack of training and development opportunities. Many reported on the lack of funding for training as budgets are now managed by schools and some schools do not prioritise TA training. Many respondents also referred to a lack of suitable and affordable options for TA training. Clearly, things are not ideal and the lack of national guidance is an issue. However, there are some courses in some areas which TAs can access.

The following qualifications are available for those not yet employed in the role:

- Level 2 Award in Support Work in Schools
- Level 3 Award in Supporting Teaching and Learning in Schools

These awards are theory based with no practical, school-based experience. If you want practical experience, you will need to ask at your local school about volunteering as a helper. If the school is agreeable, you would have to go through a series of checks to ensure that you do not have any history which might put children at risk (safeguarding procedures).

If you are a new or experienced TA you can access the following qualifications, which are available at local colleges and through apprenticeships.

- Level 3 Award in Supporting Teaching and Learning in Schools
- Level 3 Certificate Supporting Teaching and Learning in Schools
- Level 3 Diploma in Specialist Support for Teaching and Learning in Schools

These qualifications include work-based assessment.

To find out more about these qualifications see: www.education.gov.uk/schools/careers/traininganddevelopment/staff

'Skills for Schools' (skillsforschools.org) is a helpful online guide to careers, training and development in schools, developed and managed by UNISON. It has useful information on entry requirements for TAs, and also training and career development. There is also more information on the National Careers Service website: https://nationalcareersservice.direst.gov.uk.

If you are a new TA following an induction programme or an experienced TA following a training course, you will benefit from having a mentor in the form of a teacher or an experienced TA who can guide you and answer any of your questions.

Mentors

School-based mentors are important in the induction and training of teaching assistants, especially in supporting school-based tasks. While mentors have specific responsibility in this area, all teachers play their part in modelling effective learning and teaching approaches for TAs and in supporting their new learning. Discussing the implications and next steps is crucial in helping to develop the confidence and expertise of TAs and in building teams and professional working relationships.

As an assistant you can learn a great deal by watching good teachers and experienced TAs at work, and many TAs report that this is how best they learn the job. There are tried and tested ways of handling children which you can successfully copy. This works best if you ask for a particular skill to be demonstrated and talked through with you before and after the activity so that you are clear about how and why a particular approach works.

The SENCO or a class teacher probably carries the main responsibility for your day-to-day work. This responsibility should include 'on the job' training, with opportunities provided for planning and evaluation of what you do. Start by identifying together what you need to know and planning a programme to meet your needs. Ideally your staff supporter or mentor should be able to watch you at work in order to provide helpful suggestions. Of course, this can only work well when the teacher responsible is given time to do this – many school managers are now becoming aware of this need and are providing some space in the week to allow this to happen. Some schools are now asking teachers to act as mentors for assistants new to the job and in larger schools assistants form self-help groups. Training for TAs is, in one sense, an ongoing process which takes place in the school on a 'drip-feed' basis as the teacher and TA work together on a daily basis to determine ground rules, to plan programmes and to clarify responsibilities. The school has the responsibility for this aspect of training and as an assistant you have a responsibility to the pupil to ask when you are unclear about what is expected, e.g. you may be asked to work with a pupil using a computer and you may not know how to do this. Clearly, training is necessary.

What should training include?

There are several aspects of training:

- Training to understand roles and responsibilities;
- Training to understand the education and legislative framework;
- Training to understand general child development and how children learn;
- Training to understand specific skills needed to meet different learning support needs.

Induction training

All assistants benefit from induction training, which should include the following:

- respective roles and responsibilities of TAs and teachers;
- legislation including safeguarding (child protection);
- SEN Code of Practice and ILPs;
- background knowledge of the national curriculum and ways of enabling access to that curriculum;
- school policies and procedures;
- support strategies;
- developmental aspects of learning – how children learn and what makes learning difficult for some children;
- managing pupil behaviour, motivating pupils, building self-esteem, problem-solving approaches, active listening;
- supporting the development of literacy skills;
- supporting the development of numeracy skills;
- supporting the development of language skills;
- use of resources including information and communication technology;
- assessing and recording children's progress and interpreting professional assessment;
- promoting social and educational inclusion.

Training in specific skills

If you are asked to run a specific programme, e.g. for literacy development, then you will need training in how to do it effectively, following the guidelines which will be provided. If you are asked to be a learning mentor for named pupils, you will need to be trained in this role. Some TAs are trained as emotional literacy support assistants (ELSAs) and this role requires particular training and ongoing supervision.

Specialist training for special educational needs

If you are working with a pupil who has special educational needs, e.g. cerebral palsy, you may need to learn certain physiotherapy routines, or if you work with a child who has a language impairment you will need to know what particular programme is relevant and why. In these cases the physiotherapist and speech therapist respectively will be the people who can train you (and the teacher) to use the right approaches. TAs frequently ask for training in managing behaviour. The SENCO or the school's linked educational psychologist can give support in recommending ways of working with pupils who have social, emotional or behavioural difficulties.

Some local authorities have teams of advisory teachers who support children with special needs (e.g. visual impairment, hearing impairment, physical disability) and these teachers are able to support you with background information and practical advice.

In addition to basic training needs, most assistants will also need training to develop awareness, skills and strategies for supporting pupils with particular learning support needs in the following areas:

- literacy and numeracy (including dyslexia);
- speech and language, and signing;
- physical disability, motor coordination, sensory-motor and perceptual motor difficulty, including dyspraxia and cerebral palsy;
- hearing impairment;
- visual impairment;
- emotional and behavioural difficulties including AD/HD and challenging behaviour;
- autistic spectrum disorders;
- severe learning difficulties, including Down's syndrome;
- medical difficulties, e.g. epilepsy, severe asthma, terminal deteriorating conditions and bereavement issues;
- social skills, communication, use of Circle Time;
- active listening and basic counselling skills;
- working with parents;
- working with support services.

Who can best deliver this training?

A range of courses are run at many colleges and universities but some of the more tailored courses can be delivered in school. Your school SENCO will have specialist knowledge about how best to work with a wide range of specific learning needs. Sometimes training can be offered by educational practitioners, e.g. educational psychologists, specialist teachers and SENCOs, as these are the people who are working very closely with children who need learning support.

Contributions of others for specific aspects of training will be beneficial, e.g. speech and language therapists, physiotherapists, occupational therapists, paediatricians, etc.

Higher level teaching assistants

If you want to become a Higher Level Teaching Assistant (HLTA) you will need to have experience of working as a regular TA and have support from your head teacher, who will need to agree the funding and to approach training providers. HLTAs do all the things that regular TAs do but they have an increased level of responsibility, for example, they can sometimes teach classes following teacher directions or cover for planned absences. They are able to plan, prepare and deliver learning activities with groups of pupils and have more responsibility in assessing, recording and reporting on pupil progress. In addition, many HLTAs have other responsibilities, for example, they may manage other assistants, develop specialist curriculum topics or have an enhanced role in parent liaison.

To qualify as HLTA you will need the following skills and experience:

- Meet the HLTA professional standards in the government's framework.
- Have English and maths skills at Level 2 or equivalent.

- Be competent in using ICT to support your work.

- Have training in relevant strategies e.g. literacy, numeracy.

- Have specialist skills or training in a curriculum area, e.g. sign language, health and safety.

Quite a number of HLTAs decide to train as teachers. So if you're thinking of going into teaching in the long term, then working as a TA can be an excellent place to start your teaching career. You may be eligible to follow a foundation degree, available at colleges and universities and have various titles such as 'Teaching and Learning Support'. A list of courses can be found by searching under 'Teaching Assistant Studies' in the subject group section of the UCAS foundation degree website.

Useful links

Becoming a TA: Department for Education website
   www.gov.uk/department-for-education

Job profile of a TA: National Careers Website
   https://nationalcareersservice.direst.gov.uk

Information on HLTAs: HLTA programme
   hlta.org.uk

National Occupational Standards for school support staff
   https://www.gov.uk/.../NOS-for-supporting-teaching-learning

Note: In Scotland the term 'classroom assistant' and 'pupil support assistant' is used more than 'teaching assistant'. For more information contact Skills Development Scotland
   www.myworldofwork.co.uk

In Northern Ireland contact Careers Service Northern Ireland
   www.nidirect.gov.uk/careers

In Wales / Cymru contact Careers Wales
   www.careerswales.com

Activity

Professional development needs.

Working on your own, or in a pair with a TA colleague, ask the following questions.

- What is the best way that I learn new skills? e.g. courses, INSET, observing others, etc.

- What training have I had which was really useful?

- What training or development do I need to be more effective?

- How can I access this training or development?

- Which teachers can support me in getting this training?

- Is there any training or development opportunity I have found helpful that I can share with my TA colleagues?

Some final comments

As we move further towards a recognition and formalising of the positive contribution of teaching assistants (TAs), it is interesting to reflect on how far we have come in using assistance in our schools and of how the job of an assistant has changed significantly over the last 20 years. Any negative labelling, e.g. 'non-teaching assistant' has, quite rightly, become obsolete.

When I started the revision of this book, I had not appreciated just how much the role and contribution of assistants has changed. In reviewing the reports from the government and the research projects conducted over recent years and also talking to TAs in their schools, it is clear that there is a significantly greater focus on promoting academic progress alongside the more pastoral and nurturing role that TAs have traditionally undertaken. Assistants need to develop a greater understanding of how children learn and be confident enough to use their initiative in responding to individual pupil needs. TAs also need to have an appreciation of the pressures that the current culture, including social media, presents to the pupils with whom they work.

In the last ten years the potential of assistants who, in the main, support children and young people who are disadvantaged or need learning support has become increasingly recognised. Their role in promoting learning through leading small-group work following specific programmes has been highlighted as particularly effective.

Access to, and funding for, training remains an issue. With the lack of a national steer from government, much depends where you live and whether your school prioritises TA training and development. Hopefully, the next few years will see the role more clearly described and there will continue to be improvements in both training opportunities and career structure. A framework for employment and professional development, steered by the Department for Education, would be very helpful in providing standards and equal opportunities and ensuring that high-quality training is accessible for all teaching assistants. However, as this is not yet established, schools continue to have the responsibility for employment and development. As schools vary considerably in their management and have different priorities, there is still not enough consistency in the way assistants are managed and deployed. However, many schools are now addressing the issues of support and training and good schools are including TA development as part of school improvement planning.

School managers and SENCOs who employ assistants have a direct influence on, and responsibility for, the quality of TA experience in school. I hope this handbook encourages managers to think carefully and creatively about how they use this valuable resource and about how they can provide support and development opportunities.

The happiest assistants are those who are valued by their colleagues and who are clear about their roles and responsibilities. The most effective assistants in promoting academic, social and emotional progress are those who are proactively managed, deployed effectively and appropriately trained. In this handbook I have suggested ways of working together which will lead to a greater understanding of the potential of teaching assistants and improved outcomes for children and young people. I hope that it will encourage senior managers, teachers and assistants to look together at how best to support each other and how best to support the pupils with whom they work.

Above all, I hope I have given practical advice and reassurance to assistants which will enable them to be clearer about their roles and responsibilities and help them to work more confidently in supporting children, teachers and schools.

Appendix A

A job description suggestion for a teaching assistant (TA)

NB This job description is for a teaching assistant working in a mainstream school. Specific adaptations would be necessary for assistants working in special schools.

JOB TITLE:	**Teaching Assistant**
GRADE:	
RESPONSIBLE TO:	Head teacher/Class teacher/SENCO
RECEIVES INSTRUCTIONS FROM:	Head teacher/Class teacher/SENCO
PURPOSE OF JOB:	To support teachers and pupils as directed, to promote learning, achievement and well-being.

Job Duties

A Supporting the pupil

1 To help the pupil/s to learn as effectively as possible both in class and group situations, and on his/her own by, for example:

- clarifying and explaining instructions;
- ensuring the pupil is able to use equipment and materials provided;
- motivating and encouraging the pupil/s as required;
- assisting in weaker areas, e.g. language, behaviour, reading, spelling, handwriting/presentation, etc.;
- helping pupils to concentrate on and finish work set;

- meeting physical needs as required whilst encouraging independence;
- developing appropriate resources to support the pupil/s.

2 To demonstrate and develop a knowledge of a range of learning support needs and an understanding of the specific needs of the pupil/s to be supported.

3 To establish a supportive relationship with the pupil/s concerned.

4 To encourage acceptance and inclusion of all pupils, especially those who are disadvantaged or have special needs.

5 To demonstrate and develop methods of promoting/reinforcing the self-esteem and well-being of the pupil/s.

B Supporting the teacher

1 To support lessons by following the teachers' directions either in the classroom or out of the classroom as appropriate.

2 To assist, with class teacher (and other professionals as appropriate), in the development and deployment of programmes of support for pupils who need learning support.

3 In conjunction with the class teacher and/or SENCO, to support the recording of pupil/s progress.

4 To contribute to pupil progress records.

5 To participate in the evaluation of the support programme.

6 To provide regular feedback about the pupil/s to the teacher.

C Supporting the curriculum

1 To develop a knowledge of the curriculum which the pupils are expected to follow, and how progress is assessed.

2 To deliver specific programmes linked to learning, e.g. literacy and numeracy.

3 To demonstrate skills, including the use of information and communication technology, in order to adapt subject-based activities and resources to meet the needs of the pupil (in conjunction with the teacher).

D Supporting the school

1 To follow school policies and procedures.

2 To liaise, advise and consult with other members of the team supporting the pupil/s when requested.

3 To attend relevant in-service training.

4 To contribute to external reviews of pupil/s progress, as appropriate.

5 To follow guidance on safeguarding, be aware of confidential issues linked to home/pupil/teacher/school work and to keep confidences appropriately.

E Performance management

1 To take part in performance management (appraisal) annually in order to review performance, set future objectives and identify training and development needs.

Any other tasks as directed by head teacher which fall within the purview of the post.

Appendix B

The roles of supporting professionals

During the course of your work in school, it is likely that you will come across one or more of the following professionals:

Physiotherapists

The physiotherapist identifies a child's main physical problems and devises a programme of treatment to overcome them. This may include: exercises, the use of splints or other aids, and advice on seating and general classroom handling.

Occupational therapists

The occupational therapist (OT) works with children who have difficulties with gross and fine motor coordination and/or perceptual problems. The OT is concerned with a child's functional independence in all daily activities, from dressing to handwriting, and special equipment is recommended where appropriate. OTs also work in child guidance services and can help with some emotional and psychological needs.

Speech and language therapists (SALTs)

Speech and language therapists work with children who may have a wide range of disorders affecting their understanding and use of speech and/or language. They will assess the child's progress and provide a programme of activities aimed at developing listening skills, use of speech sounds, development of sentence structure, etc.

Educational psychologists

Educational psychologists visit most schools on a regular basis in order to support children and the adults who work with them. They are called on to help and advise on a variety of emotional and educational problems. They may also devise programmes and carry out individual assessments. In addition, they write psychological advice as part of education, health and care plans. They also work with schools to develop policies and practices, e.g. behaviour management.

Teacher advisers

As the title suggests, teacher advisers give advice to class teachers on specific issues. In addition, they may teach or assess individual children. Each teacher is usually a specialist in a specific area, e.g. learning difficulties, hearing impairment, physical disability, visual impairment, etc.

School medical officers (community paediatricians)

School medical officers are doctors who visit schools on a regular basis in order to see all children at certain stages in their school lives, and particular children as the need arises. They are able to provide diagnosis and to give advice about the medical implications of certain conditions.

Social workers

You may come into contact with social workers if you attend a case conference or multi-agency meeting about a child you support. Their role is to report and advise on family and housing issues affecting the child.

Appendix C

Glossary of abbreviations

You will come across a considerable number of abbreviations in the course of your work. Here are some of the more common ones:

AfL	Assessment for Learning
ADD	Attention Deficit Disorder
AD/HD	Attention Deficit/Hyperactivity Disorder
AFASIC	Association for all Speech Impaired Children
AIDS	Acquired Immune Deficiency Syndrome
AR	Annual Review
ARE	Age Related Expectations
ASD	Autistic Spectrum Disorders
AT	Attainment Targets
BSS	Behaviour Support Service
CDT	Craft, Design and Technology
CEO	County Education Officer/Chief Education Officer
CF	Cystic Fibrosis
CMO	Clinical Medical Officer
COP	Code of Practice
CP	Cerebral Palsy
CPD	Continuing Professional Development
DfE	Department for Education
EAL	English as an Additional Language
EBSD	Emotional Behavioural and Social Difficulties
EHCP	Education, Health and Care Plan
EP	Educational Psychologist
EWO	Education Welfare Officer
EYFS	Early Years Foundation Stage
FSM	Free School Meals
GCSE	General Certificate of Secondary Education
GNVQ	General National Vocational Qualification
G & T	Gifted and Talented
HI	Hearing Impairment
HIV	Human Immunodeficiency Virus

HLTA	Higher Level Teaching Assistant
HMI	Her Majesty's Inspector
HOF	Head of Faculty
HOY	Head of Year
IBP	Individual Behaviour Plan
ICT	Information and Communication Technology
IEP	Individual Education Plan
ILP	Individual Learning Programme
INSET	In-Service Training
LA	Local Authority
LAC	Looked After Child(ren)
LSA	Learning Support Assistant
MDA	Multi-Disciplinary Assessment
ME	Myalgic Encephalomyelitis (Chronic Fatigue Syndrome)
MFL	Modern Foreign Languages
MLD	Moderate Learning Difficulties
MO	Medical Officer
MS	Multiple Sclerosis
NQT	Newly Qualified Teacher
NVQ	National Vocational Qualification
Ofsted	Office for Standards in Education
OT	Occupational Therapist
PMLD	Profound and Multiple Learning Difficulties
PP	Pupil Premium
PPA	Planning, Preparation and Assessment
PSHE	Personal, Social and Health Education
PSP	Pastoral Support Plan
PTA	Parent Teacher Association
SALT	Speech and Language Therapist
SDP	School Development Plan
SEN	Special Educational Needs
SENCO	Special Educational Needs Coordinator
SLD	Severe Learning Difficulties
SLP	Student Learning Profile
SLT	Senior Leadership Team
SMT	Senior Management Team
SpLD	Specific Learning Difficulties
VI	Visual Impairment

References

Ainscow, M. and Tweddle, D. A. (1988) *Encouraging Classroom Success.* London: David Fulton Publishers.

Audit Commission/HMI. (1992a) *Getting in on the Act: A Management Handbook for Schools and LEAs.* London: HMSO.

Audit Commission/HMI. (1992b) *Getting the Act Together.* London: HMSO.

Balshaw, M. H. (1991) *Help in the Classroom.* London: David Fulton Publishers.

Bennett, A. (1985) 'Meeting the Integration Needs of Partially Hearing Unit Pupils'. *AEP Journal* 6 (5).

Code of Practice on the Identification and Assessment of Special Educational Needs. (2015) DfE and Welsh Office.

Code of Practice in Special Educational Needs. (2001) DfES publications.

Cooper, P. and Ideus, K. (1996) *Attention Deficit/Hyperactivity Disorder: A Practical Guide for Teachers.* London: David Fulton Publishers.

Department for Education. (2013) 'School Workforce in England: November 2013'. Available online at www.gov.uk/government/statistics/school-workforce-in-england-november-2013

Department for Education. (2014) 'Supporting Pupils at Schools with Medical Conditions'. Available online at www.gov.uk/government/publications/supporting-pupils-at-school-with-medical-conditions--3

Department for Education. (2015a) 'Keeping Children Safe in Education'. Available online at www.gov.uk/government/publications/keeping-children-safe-in-education--2

Department for Education. (2015b) 'Schools, Pupils and their Characteristics: January 2015'. Available online at www.gov.uk/government/statistics/schools-pupils-and-their-characteristics-january-2015

Department for Education. (2015c) 'The Prevent Duty: Departmental Advice for Schools and Childcare Providers'. Available online at www.safeguardinginschools.co.uk/prevent-duty-guidance-from-the-dfe-july-2015/

Department for Education and Employment. (1997) 'Excellence for All Children: Meeting Special Educational Needs'. Available online at www.education.gov.uk/consultations/downloadableDocs/45_1.pdf

Department for Education and Skills. (2005) 'The Effective Management of Teaching Assistants to Improve Standards in Literacy and Mathematics'. Primary National Strategy. DfES 1228-2005. Available online at www.schoolslinks.co.uk/EffectiveManagmentOfTeachingAssistants.pdf

Dweck, Carole. (2008) *Mindset: The New Psychology of Success.* USA: Random House.

Farrell, Peter, Balshaw, Maggie, and Polat, Filiz (2000) 'The Management, Role and Training of Learning Support Assistants'. DfEE Research Report 161. Available online at webarchive.nationalarchives.gov.uk/20130401151715/http://www.education.gov.uk/publications/eOrderingDownload/RR161.pdf

Fletcher-Campbell, F. (1992) 'How Can We Use an Extra Pair of Hands?' *British Journal of Special Education,* 19 (4), 141–143.

Fox, G. and Halliwell, M. (2000) *Supporting Literacy and Numeracy.* London: David Fulton Publishers.

Haddon, M. (2003) *The Curious Incident of the Dog in the Night-Time.* London: Jonathon Cape.

Hampshire Education Authority. *Principles of Good Practice – A Tool for Self-Evaluation.* (1992) Guidelines produced by the Hampshire Inspection and Advisory Support Service.

Halliwell, M. (2003) *Supporting Children with Special Educational Needs.* London: David Fulton Publishers.

Maines, B. and Robinson, G. (2002) *You Can: You Know You Can.* Course handbook to accompany workshops on the self-concept approach. Bristol: Lucky Duck Publishing.

Mallon, B. (1987) *An Introduction to Counselling Skills for Special Educational Needs.* Manchester: Manchester University Press.

'Mending Young Minds'. (November 2015) BBC Radio 4.

Ofsted. (2000) 'Evaluating Educational Inclusion: Guidance for Inspectors and Schools'. Ofsted. Available online at http://dera.ioe.ac.uk/4455/

Rieser, R. (1994) *Developing a Whole School Approach to Inclusion*. Available from Disability Equality in Education, 78 Mildmay Grove, London N1 4PJ.

Ripley, K., Daines, B. and Barrett, J. (1997) *Dyspraxia: A Guide for Teachers and Parents*. London: David Fulton Publishers.

Royal National Institute for the Blind. (2014) 'Local Authority VI Education Service Provision for Blind and Partially Sighted Children and Young People in 2013'. Available online at www.rnib.org.uk/knowledge-and-research-hub/research-reports/education-research/vi-service-provision

Russell, A., Webster, R. and Blatchford, P. (2013) *Maximising the Impact of Teaching Assistants*. London: Routledge.

Sharples, Jonathan, Webster, Ron and Blatchford, Peter. (March 2015) Making Best Use of Teaching Assistants; Guidance Report. Education Endowment Foundation. Available online at https://v1.educationendowment foundation.org.uk/uploads/pdf/TA_Guidance_Report_Interactive.pdf

Special Educational Needs and Disability Act. (2001) Available online at www.legislation.gov.uk/ukpga/2001/10/pdfs/ukpga_20010010_en.pdf

TELLUS survey: National Foundation for Education Research. *(nfer)*

The Health Behaviour of School-Aged Children Survey [2009–10] (HBCS).

The Primary National Strategy Report, *The Effective Management of Teaching Assistants in Literacy and Mathematics in Year 6* (DfES 0340-2004).

Training and Development Agency. (2010) *Effective Deployment of School Staff*.

UNICEF Office of Research. (2013) 'Child Well-Being in Rich Countries: A Comparative Overview'. Innocenti Report Card 11, UNICEF Office of Research, Florence.

Unison. (2013) Teaching Assistants: A Class Act. Available online at www.unison.org.uk/content/uploads/2014/09/TowebTA-Survey-2013-PDF2.pdf

The Warnock Report. (1978) 'Report of the Committee of Handicapped Children and Young People'. London: HMSO.